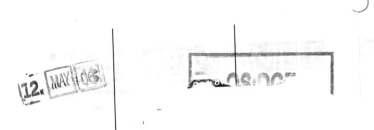

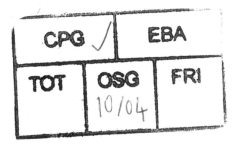

CPG ✓	EBA
TOT	OSG 10/04	FRI

A Spoonful of Rice with Salt

The author.

A Spoonful of Rice with Salt

by

George Patterson

The Pentland Press Limited
Edinburgh · Cambridge · Durham

© G. S. Patterson 1993

First published in 1993 by
The Pentland Press Ltd.
1 Hutton Close
South Church
Bishop Auckland
Durham

Reprinted 1995

ISBN 1 85821 073 9 $9/_{0k}$

Typeset by Elite Typesetting Techniques, Southampton.
Printed and bound by Antony Rowe Ltd., Chippenham.

Acknowledgements

This book was started for my wife and daughters Linda and Diana; without their encouragement it might not have been finished. I am grateful to Anne for her help with the proof reading and to Clive Dickinson for his advice during the last two years.

Contents

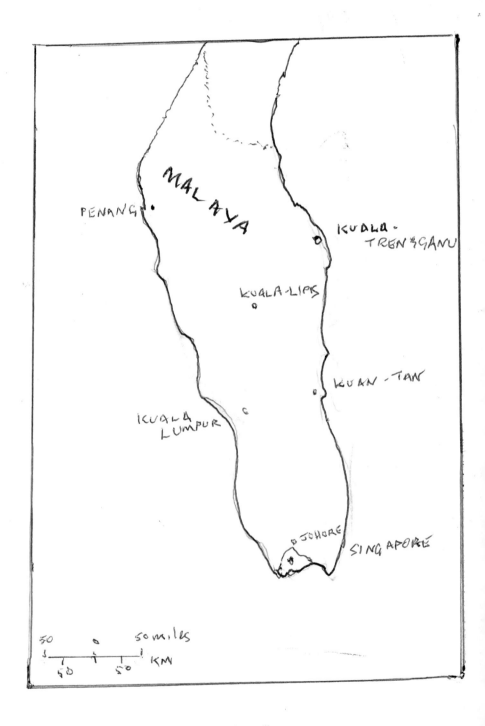

MALAYA

PENANG

KUALA-TRENGGANU

KUALA-LIPIS

KUAN-TAN

KUALA LUMPUR

JOHORE

SINGAPORE

50   0   50 miles

50   50   KM

List of Illustrations

Introduction

I first met my husband in 1945 soon after he had returned from his time as a Japanese P.O.W. He went back to Malaya in 1946 to work for Malcolm MacDonald and it was two years before we saw each other again. After a short engagement we were married in 1948.

Our first posting in Malaya was to Kota Tinggi just as the Emergency began. Our elder daughter, Linda, was born there and Diana some years later in Kuala Lumpur. We had an interesting and happy life in that lovely country and were sorry to leave when the time came for George to retire in 1960. During all this time he refused to talk about his time as a prisoner of war. One thing that I did notice was the fact that even a playful pat on his face produced an uncharacteristic reaction – so often had he been forced to kneel while the Japanese guards beat him about the head.

After we had been home for some time, the odd anecdote about his time in captivity came out and the family was sufficiently amused by some of the stories to suggest that he should write a book. George agreed to consider this once he had retired and thought it would be much easier if he had kept a diary, as he did not think he could remember enough to justify a book.

It was then that I produced his diary, an address book, two cookery books, the letters he had written home to his parents and the letters they had sent to him in P.O.W. camp. His mother, who was a methodical, well organised person, had kept them all in the bottom drawer of her desk. She died in 1962 but they did not come to light until I found them after the death of his father, Sir John Patterson, in 1976.

When I produced them, George had absolutely no idea that he had managed to keep a diary – and to get it home. All the papers formed the basis of this book.

As a family we have always loved Eastern food. It was some time before I noticed that, when we had rice, at the end of his meal George would take a spoonful of plain rice, put salt on it and eat it in silence. Thinking how fortunate he was to be able to choose what he ate. Hence the title of this book.

Anne Patterson
Farnham, January 1993

Chapter 1

Voyage to Malaya

'Why,' many people may ask, 'have you chosen to write about events which took place fifty years ago?' My reasons are complex and not easy to put down on paper. Firstly, I have been encouraged to do so by my family; my daughters have often expressed interest in what happened in prison camp and kept saying, 'Do write a book about it all.'

I have found it difficult to accept that Japan is now one of the strongest economies in the world, while our country languishes in the second division and the sacrifices made by many of my friends have gone for nought. I suppose I was influenced by the death of Emperor Hirohito and the criticism, which I thought was grossly unfair, of Prince Philip's presence at his funeral. No matter how much one reads on the subject, it is difficult to determine how responsible the Emperor was for starting the war – or indeed how much influence he exercised in bringing hostilities to an end. There can be no doubt that he was closely involved in the detailed conduct of the conflict.

The story really started when I said that I would find it easier to write a book if I had kept a diary. 'Well,' said my wife, 'you did.' My mother had kept all the letters I wrote home and on my release I must have given her my diary and note books. The little Charles Letts pocket diary and all the letters were found by my wife after my father died and we were clearing out our old home in the Lake District. I must admit that, after my release, all I wanted to do was to forget the previous four years and to get down to living a new life in a free society. I still do not remember how I managed to keep the diary and to conceal it during the many searches to which we were subjected. There were many things about the Japanese which I did not understand; one was their obsession about people keeping diaries unless they already had a sense of guilt and were afraid that the

1

prisoners were recording the names of the Japanese responsible for the atrocities.

I suppose the story really starts when I decided I would follow my father and join the Colonial Civil Service. He had a distinguished career in Nigeria, a country barred to me by the sensible rule that sons should not serve in the same territory as their fathers – at the same time. I went up to Oxford to read chemistry but, as the war had started, continued with my military activities, leading to a Certificate B. Having volunteered at the outbreak of war, I was called up and subsequently commissioned in the Royal Artillery after a torrid time at O.C.T.U. in Catterick during the awful winter of 1940. Soon after I was commissioned, I was called to a Colonial Service interview and asked where I would like to serve – apart from Nigeria. It was a difficult choice for a young man to make; I was only twenty and knew little about overseas territories. The Sudan and Malaya both wanted cadets so I put my name down for both countries. After some weeks I got my orders to join a ship in Glasgow for a journey to Malaya.

Malaya was then a major supplier of rubber and tin and the thinking was that the administration should be reinforced at all costs. My mother went to Glasgow with me as she had relatives in that city and we stayed with them the night before I boarded the S.S. *Ulysses*, a Blue Funnel ship of about 20,000 tons and a certain age.

Everything was blacked out and we sailed in the darkness; it was an imposing sight when we woke up next morning to find ourselves in the middle of a huge convoy. There were ships as far as the eye could see. Destroyer escorts buzzed backwards and forwards, encouraging the laggards and keeping the faster ships on station. Even though it was midsummer, it was miserably cold as we steamed north towards the Arctic Circle.

When the war started, my mother moved from our home near Newcastle across to the Lake District with another family, The Grants, as the school attended by my brother and the Grant boys was evacuated to Penrith. Commodore Grant, R.N.R., had been called from his appointment with the Canadian Pacific Line to a senior post in the Admiralty. He never told my mother where I was but he was able to assure her now and again that I was still above water rather than under the sea.

It was a miserable crossing of the Atlantic, even in July, as we steered a course as far north as possible. Finally we arrived at a port which turned out to be Halifax in Nova Scotia. We were not allowed ashore, presumably for security reasons, and having taken on board fuel (coal) and supplies we set sail for Durban. We hugged the coasts of North and South America as the German pocket battleships, the *Sharnhorst* and the *Gneisneau* were on the prowl, sinking everything in sight. It was at this time that the Captain called for volunteers for submarine watch and for a few weeks I did my stint in the hot sun, scanning the horizon and hoping to see nothing hostile.

Life on board had settled down to a pleasant routine, considering all the circumstances, and I made many friends. I could understand it was necessary for wives to accompany senior service and civilian officers but, for the life of me, I could not see why young R.A.F. wives were being shipped out to join their husbands in Ceylon. They were an attractive collection and provided light relief for the young men on board.

It seemed an age before we finally got to Durban and, for the first time in seven weeks, were allowed ashore. The ship was taking on coal and I can't remember anything quite as horrific as the dust which settled on everything. The voyage had lasted much longer than I had anticipated and I was extremely short of money but that did not prevent me from having the largest grilled sole that I have ever seen. The food on board had been very reasonable but water was getting very short and it is hell in the tropics if you can't wash the smalls. At Durban I was able to post my first letter home.

At Sea.
Sunday 6th July 1941

I hope you will excuse this being written in pencil, my pen has run out and there is never any ink in the inkwells because of the evaporation.

I have been meaning to write to you for a long time but since the weather became warmer we have had a lot more to do on board. We have been in the Tropics for a few days now but we have always had a breeze which makes the high temperatures bearable. The only time we feel really hot is at night because the portholes must be kept closed and there are four of us in a double cabin.

I hope you got my last letter and cable, I'm sorry to have to ask for more money but the trip can't be done easily on £10. I am drinking very little and cigarettes are only 1/9d for fifty but laundry is heavy and my bill is usually about 18/- each week.

I am sharing a cabin with three other chaps who are going out as Cadet Police Officers. Two are fine fellows but the third is a bit difficult and spends much of his spare time lifting weights. Simon Simpson was Oxford's full-back and I met him with Denis Melrose, whom you may remember was wounded in that shooting affair at University College. Simon was offered an administrative appointment in Sierra Leone but turned it down and is now wondering whether he did the right thing. I personally would rather be in Sierra Leone than the Malayan Police. The other chap is an amusing Scotsman from St. Andrews called Maclean.

On board is an Admiral Spooner whose wife was Miss Megan Foster the singer and this morning she gave a recital which lasted just under an hour. She has a beautiful voice and I think everyone enjoyed it; the Admiral himself accompanied her. He, by the way is a relative of the great Spooner, Warden of New College.

I have had some very interesting talks with Lady Northcote whose husband is Governor of Hong Kong and she is going out to join him. Her sons were at Balliol and we have had some grand discussions about Oxford. She says that after about ten years in a Colony one should take any chance of a transfer on promotion that comes one's way. She has been all over the place – Gold Coast, East Africa, Trinidad and somewhere else I can't remember before Hong Kong. She also advises that one should wangle one's way into the Secretariat.

Many people have been ill with sunburn but I have managed to keep out of the sun and am going a beautiful even brown. I do an hour a day on submarine watch and the time advances by one hour each day. Tomorrow I do 12.00 noon to 1.00 p.m. and since we are just on the equator it is pretty hot; I cover myself up and wear a steel helmet which has an air space and is remarkably comfortable.

20th Sunday

One of the many rumours on the ship is that we shall be able to post letters in a few days. It is over four weeks since we came on board, with the prospect of another six weeks to Singapore. The laundry has now ceased to function because of the shortage of water; it is turned off at various hours during the day and the amount allowed for a bath is very small indeed.

Our next port of call was Colombo and there I had an introduction to Mr. and Mrs. Meaden; she was an aunt of Mrs. Grant, sharing a house with my parents. Mr. Meaden was the Chairman of E. Johns & Co., a major import and export house. It was here that I saw my first example of 'life in the East': the Meaden house was set in beautiful grounds and Mrs. Meaden had the most marvellous collection of antiques. Air conditioning was in its infancy but the Meaden treasures were protected by the most modern equipment available. Servants seemed to be everywhere and at dinner that evening one stood behind each diner's chair; it was luxury that I had read about but thought it was confined to the palaces of kings and princes. To make conversation, I remember saying that it must have taken a lot of work to keep the brass badges in their headgear so bright. I was rocked back on my heels when I heard that the badges were nine carat gold. The Meadens were wonderful to an impressionable young man and I left them with happy memories – and £10 to help me out of my financial problems.

I have often tried to analyse my first impressions of 'The East'. Colombo was noisy and smelly. On the dockside small characters were shouting, milling about, going in all directions with no apparent end in view. Until you have stood on a quayside in the east, you cannot appreciate the scents of the herbs which float on the breezes. I left Colombo in a state of moderate shock but feeling that I might have arrived close to the career that I had chosen – little as I knew about it at long range.

After a brief call in Penang we arrived in Singapore. The voyage had taken ten weeks and four days, which is slightly longer than the seventeen hours by Singapore Airlines 747 jets. From the discussions I had had with Dick Middleton-Smith during the trip, I had decided to try to get an appointment on the Malay side – rather than learn Chinese or an Indian language. The officers who learnt a Chinese dialect stayed for some years in the Chinese Secretariat; those who went to India to learn a language of that huge continent worked in the Labour Department. Their main task was to ensure the labourers on the rubber estates were well treated, with all the problems associated with their employment. I had determined that I would do everything to try to become a Malay Cadet. Chinese is a tonal language and to learn it musical ability is useful. When I was asked if I was musical I replied in the negative – even though I had managed to play in the orchestra at school. I never regretted that white lie.

Airmail was expensive as my first letter home from Singapore indicated.

c/o Malayan Establishment Office,
Singapore.
Tuesday 26th August 1941

My dear Mother,

Firstly I must impress upon you to read this letter with due reverence, it comes by Clipper and cost me two dollars, which is near enough to five shillings to make one think about wasting space. I am writing it in stages because I have a lot to tell you.

We arrived here on Friday and I had no orders at all and nobody came on board to meet me. Middleton-Smith went ashore for breakfast and then came to collect me in his car. Together we went to see the Malayan Establishment Officer called Peel [subsequently Sir John Peel, M.P. for Leicester and Euro M.P.] whose younger brother is an Assistant District Officer in Nigeria. He said that he knew I was coming but he had no exact date and no firm posting had been arranged for me. He arranged for me to go into the Adelphi Hotel and for my baggage to be collected from the ship. Peel is the third Establishment Officer and he took me to see Mr. Shean, who is in charge of the Department. He suggested that I might like to learn Chinese but I told him I was not very keen so he said that I should go into the Cadets Bungalow and not stay in the hotel. I must say the bungalow is very comfortable, with excellent food, and the chaps living here are very decent. They have taken me all over the place and I come in with them in their cars every morning. The place is quite a long way out, about six miles, and stands on a cliff overlooking the harbour. I am sharing one of their boys; he looks after Philip Wickens, who is Private Secretary to the Colonial Secretary, Mr. Jones.

On Saturday I ordered my white clothes which were delivered on Monday, tailor made and very smart. These Chinese certainly know their jobs.

On Saturday I came into the Secretariat Office and had a look round. Wickens, who is a New College man, introduced me to the Under Secretary, Mr. Ward; he is a charming man and knew that my father was in the service. He, in turn, took me to see the Colonial Secretary, Mr. Jones. He has a terrific amount of work these days but talked to me for a few minutes.

Yesterday I came into the Secretariat for the first time as a worker. I have a beautiful big desk but no clearly defined job. I am finding my way about code books and learning a little Malay. I heard yesterday that I am going up to Trengganu on the East Coast to the British Advisers Office. Trengganu is an Unfederated State and quite near Thailand. A cadet had been up there for a year and is now being moved, I am quite lucky to be going there because I will have ample opportunity to get to know the Malays and learn the language. The Adviser always wants a Private Secretary and I think I will be acting in that capacity but there is not an immense amount of work and I will have plenty of time to do my language and law. Wickens got through his exams in eleven months so I'm going to have a good crack at mine. I met the Legal Adviser from Trengganu yesterday and he says he thinks I will like the place; he very kindly undertook to arrange for me to stay with the District Officer or with an engineer called Jerome. Both, I believe are very good chaps, so I should be very comfortable. There are only about sixty Europeans in the District and living should be fairly cheap. Fortunately I don't think I will need a car, they are terribly expensive here and rationing is in force for petrol. The District, I believe, is very attractive with beautiful white beaches and hard firm sand. The other cadets say I am very lucky to be going there so early because I will have a good chance to learn Malay.

Middleton-Smith is working in the Secretariat as second assistant secretary and on Friday night we went to dinner with Peel. He is married and his wife is very charming. We had a beautiful meal and spent a very pleasant evening. Also there were a Mr. and Mrs. Evans; he is an auditor now serving with the R.A.F. and was for some time in Kano where he knew Dad.

As you know, I saw Mr. and Mrs. Meaden in Colombo and he lent me £10, which he would like paid into his wife's account in England. He is a fine old chap and I had a very pleasant time with them. I stayed the night, arriving at about seven, and left at ten the next morning. They were very interested in all the family chat and the war but it is a great strain having to shout so much as Mrs. Meaden is so very deaf. They have a marvellous place, like a small palace with a most imposing porch and entrance. When I got there they had a drink and sandwiches ready and we talked until dinner at 8.15. I saw the house on a tour of inspection and this took a long time because there is so much beautiful stuff. From what little I know about china and gold plate, the place must be worth a fortune. Some of the furniture, especially the French tapestry suite, is most impressive – it is all in a room which measures thirty yards by fifteen yards!! There are numerous boys rushing about the place and one never needs to lift a finger. When I came away Mrs. Meaden gave me eight new books which she had just read – they will be very useful where I am going. I wanted to get up early to go with him to see his fruit farm but Mrs. Meaden would not agree and I had breakfast with her. She has some hens at the back of the house where they used to keep their race horses and these seem to carry off most of the prizes at the shows. She told me that the prize-winners all had rings on their legs and it was difficult to pick out a bird that was not so adorned. Do tell Aunt Doris (Grant) about all this, I'm sure she will be interested.

Thursday 28th August

I'm afraid I have not been able to add much to this letter because I have actually been working. I have been in the Colonial Secretary's office doing some work and seeing how the filing system works. Today I have been in the taxation department and may be required to organise the work, under supervision of course, when I go up-country. It takes a bit of understanding but I hope to get the hang of things in the few days that remain before I depart.

Today I went to see the Governor, Sir Shenton Thomas, and was with him for about half an hour. He is a charming man and put me very much at ease; he remembered Dad and asked me to send kindest regards when next I wrote. He said I was very lucky to be going to Trengganu and hoped I would make the most of the opportunities that would be offered.

Tonight I had my first game of tennis with Mr. Peel. He has a lovely house with a tennis court; four of us managed to get in three sets before it became too dark to play. The other two were Black, the Controller of Foreign Exchange, and a Colonel Palmer – I don't know his regiment but I will find out. We had a good game and I feel much better for the exercise but the sea trip has not made me any fitter. I wish I had been in better form.

Please tell all and sundry the news in this letter; included is a note for brother Hugh but I can't write to everyone. I will write by the next Clipper, the service goes once a fortnight so I will be able to afford a letter to you every time and to others when I feel very rich!! The living up-country should be quite cheap so I can afford to let you have the news by the quickest possible means.

Your loving son.

Chapter 2

To Trengganu

So I had achieved my ambition and was to be posted to a Malay State in a very junior administrative role. It is probably useful at this moment in the story to say something about the geography and complex political structure of the country.

Malaya is a small country, about 500 miles long and 200 miles across at its broadest point; Singapore sits as a small island at its southern extremity. It is about a degree north of the equator and generally the climate is hot and wet. Things have changed but, before the war, only the west side of Malaya was fully developed; the railway ran from Singapore to the Siamese border. There was no east coast road, progress was slow as each river had to be crossed by ferry – usually manhandled. The western plain was rich in tin mines and vast rubber estates of the highest quality. The hills in the centre of the country run down it like a spine, rising to 3,000 feet at the highest point. It was over this range that I walked when the Japanese attacked in December 1941.

The political structure was complex and, to a young man of twenty-one, difficult to grasp. There were three Crown Colonies, Singapore, Penang and Malacca, where the administration was 'direct', that is to say, the British officers decided the last word. There were a number of Federated States and Unfederated States which were administered 'indirectly'; the states were tied to the United Kingdom by treaty. Briefly the two subjects over which the U.K. had ultimate authority were defence and foreign affairs. The senior British officers were entitled Residents in the Federated States but Advisers in the Unfederated States.

The population of Singapore is predominantly Chinese. The Malays are the major race in Malaya, working in Government service and owning small estates throughout the country. Chinese ran the small village shops and many of the large enterprises in the towns. The Indians, apart from some shopkeepers, were to be found on the rubber estates where they provided most of the labour. This is probably too simple a description and does not reflect the situation that prevails in Malaysia at the present time, but it was as the situation seemed to me all those years ago.

Each state had its own Sultan and state council. Perhaps the best known Sultan was the colourful and immensely wealthy Sultan of Johore who, I believe, gave the R.A.F. money from his own personal fortune to buy three Spitfires. Islam is the official religion of the country. When I arrived in Trengganu I found that we were on holiday Thursday afternoons and Fridays; the central secretariat in Kuala Lumpur took Saturday afternoon and Sunday as rest days. As my British Adviser pointed out, 'If you can arrange to go on tour on Monday and Tuesday, it only leaves one day when K.L. can get at you.'

My purpose in setting out this complex administrative set-up is to emphasise how difficult some of the decisions became when war broke out. We were there as the protecting power, Malaya was not 'owned' by the U.K. but, as it was to prove, failure to protect it meant disastrous consequences.

My first journey in that wonderful country was a real experience. I had never seen such lush vegetation, the rubber estates came right down to the railway track. The speed of the train enabled one to get a very good look at everything that went on in the villages so close to the line. My journey took me close to the Siamese border before completing the next part by road, turning southeast to Trengganu. My next letter to my father describes my arrival. I did have problems because my mother and brother were still in England, but my father was in Nigeria and I was anxious that they should get my news as quickly as possible.

Kuala Trengganu
2nd September 1941

My dear Dad,
Thank you for your letter posted on August 12th which arrived in Singapore on the 30th, the day before I left to come up here. Mum's letters seem to be taking a terrible time, I'm hoping to get mine home in a fortnight or three weeks. I was expecting some letters when I arrived but haven't heard anything.

On Saturday evening I caught the train to come up here. They are extremely comfortable and I had a berth, sleeping until nine o'clock the next morning. It is a narrow gauge and not very fast so I saw quite a lot of the States of Pahang and Kelantan. We arrived at Kuala Krai at 3.30 on Sunday afternoon and I was met by the Station Master who spoke very good English. He had, on the instructions of the British Adviser, arranged for a car and a lorry to take my baggage. The lorry went straight to Trengganu while I went to Besut to stay the night with Marsh, the District Officer. The roads are quite good and I saw a lot of the countryside, the kampongs, villages, are all along the sides of the roads and you can see the people going about their everyday activities.

Smith, whose place I am taking, came up to Besut and I came here on Monday morning while he went on to Krai. I suppose the journey was about 130 miles. The idea was that Smith should tell me about the place and give me some advice. I found him singularly uncommunicative and got no information from him whatsoever. He is rather a superior young man and tried to make me promise to continue the projects in which he had been interested.

I arrived here about midday on Monday and went straight to the Residency where I met Mr. de Moubray, the British Adviser, and Mrs. de Moubray. They are a charming couple and I'm sure I'm going to enjoy myself here. I am living in a little bungalow in the Residency grounds and will have all my meals in the Residency. The bungalow has two bedrooms, each with a bathroom and pushbutton, there is a veranda and I am writing this letter sitting on it.

I have not done much except to see how things are organised and I've seen some of the Town and offices. I am going to press on with my Malay and had my first lesson with my 'munshi' yesterday. He is a good man and speaks English quite well so that he can explain things when I am in doubt. I find that I can understand a fair amount of any conversation but I am not quick enough to think of the words myself.

The day I arrived I went out on an exercise with the Local Defence Force, it started at 3.00 p.m. and I got back to the Residency at midnight. We marched a good way and I felt pretty tired the next morning.

Today I went to see some of the local industry of dyeing and weaving; some of the cloth is very beautiful and they have one in which is woven a gold thread. This is, of course, very expensive but it is most impressive. I am going to help with the dyeing and it should be interesting, the substance used needs a diazotisation so I am in my element.

The Residency is about 200 yards from the sea and we get lovely cooling breezes, the compound is big but on one side of the house there is a beautiful little garden where one can sit. It is screened off by a fencing that was originally put up as a protection against the monsoon. This is due soon and everyone says that the floods this year will be very big. Science and local talk seem to support this view: it appears to be a ten-year cycle and 1931 was a bad year.

I had my first game of golf with the B.A. He plays a lot and is very good but I found it difficult to hit a ball. The course is nine holes but I found the greens very tricky; because of the large amount of sand one is allowed to tee up every shot. I am so used to taking a little turf that my shots were undercut and then topped – I suppose I will get it taped sometime.

My 'boy' turned up yesterday and he seems to be a good proposition, his salary is $20 per month, which is about £2.10s.0d. His name is Mat Kechil, the 'kechil' meaning 'little' because the head boy in the Residency is called Mat. In the same way the new cadet is called the 'Tuan kechil baharu' or the new little tuan. I'm afraid he does not have much to do at the moment but if I go into a bungalow of my own he will not be so unemployed. I don't know how things will work out; there are not many Europeans here and I may be able to go and live with one of them.

I am afraid that this letter has been on my table for quite a long time. I tried to finish it but suddenly found that I was actually working; most of the work deals with files but, not having much experience with these things, it takes me rather longer than other people to find the appropriate file.

It looks very much as though I will have to get a car and I wondered if you could lend me the money. I can borrow from the Government but it has to be paid back within a certain time and I am still paying back the advance I took in England. I think £100 will be ample, cars are very expensive here but I hope I can get a small one cheaper than they will be in a year's time. If I am going to live in the next house that becomes vacant it will be some distance from the office. My first job is likely to be an investigation into the secondary industries of the State and I will need a car for my travels.

All the people in this place are very charming and I have been out to dinner quite a few nights. It is very informal and I wear white suits but in the Residency it is black tie every night. The B.A. wears Malayan silks and I am considering these because they are so much cooler. There are no ties to tie and I think I can soon learn to wind a sarong so that my trousers do not fall down.

Your affectionate son.

Looking back on it, I believe that my time in Trengganu before the war with Japan was one of the happiest periods of my life. The de Moubrays had a son about my age still in England and adopted me as their own. I could not have had a more sympathetic tutor than the B.A. himself nor a more understanding 'foster mother' than his wife. I lived in that little bungalow in the Residency grounds and took all my meals with them as part of the family. My only great regret is that this wonderful life came to such an awful end after a matter of weeks. Meanwhile I tried to convey to my parents the fascinating aspects of my new life.

c/o The British Adviser,
Kuala Trengganu.
18th September 1941

My dear Mum,

I have been trying for days to find time to write to you but all my days seem to be filled from the moment I get up until the time I go to bed. Today I have decided not to play any games so the usual two hours after tea will be spent writing.

Your very welcome letter arrived three days ago, having started out on July 3rd. Also one from David which you had redirected by the same mail but his was posted on July 16th. I wonder if you also wrote by that mail as it is not like you to miss the chance of getting a letter away. I will answer yours first before I tell you about my life up here.

I too am glad that we had to say goodbye quickly, I had to go so we may as well make the best of things. I am, as you say, very young but the training you and Dad have given me makes me feel secure in starting my career so early. [At the age of twenty-one I was two or three years younger than the normal entrant to the Malayan Civil Service.]

What a shame about my tennis racquet, the old one here smashed up and I had to buy a new one. It is made in Australia and cost only $17 (about £2) for a tournament model.

I don't think I have much more to answer in your letter; I hope the next one will contain more details about my finances. I am going to stay on in the Residency, Mr. and Mrs. de Moubray seem to like me and have said they would like me to stay. I thought of getting a house of my own but that would be expensive and Mrs. B.A. will not let me pay more than $50 a month towards my keep because the house is provided by the Government. This means I am saving about $300 per month as my cigarette and drinks bill at the Club is very small. I have written to Dad asking him to lend me £100 to buy a car as I can't go round in the Residency car as the B.A. uses it a great deal.

Last week from Wednesday to Friday I went on a trip with Jeram, the Chief Surveyor. We went to Kemaman, which is about 100 miles due south, about food control, etc. The road is new, red laterite, single track with grass growing in the middle. At one point the gradient is 1 in 5 and the road runs along the side of a cliff with no barricade. Jeram's car is a Ford V8 30 which took it easily. We stayed Wednesday night in the Rest House in Kemaman and Thursday night in Dungun, which is about forty miles from here. On Friday we played cricket, Kuala Trengganu v. Dungun. It was an amusing game, the first ever played in Dungun. We played on matting and most of the population turned out to see the mad people who played all day in the sun apart from a two-hour break for lunch. I got the usual 'O' but redeemed myself by keeping wicket and getting two stumped and not letting a single bye past me. My Malay improved on the trip because so few people speak English.

This week I have met the Sultan and his wife, known as the Tungku Ampuan; they came to tea a few days ago. Last night their son and some other people came to play darts after dinner. He is about my age and called Tungku Aziz, he was wearing the most beautiful Cambridge blue silks with a lovely sarong. (The Malay dress consists of trousers, a shirt and a sarong usually in a different cloth.) I am having my Malay clothes woven in blue shot with red. I have dyed the silk myself in the dyeing factory of which I am now the supervisor and attempting to put it on a paying basis. Brother Hugh should be here to see me haggling with the men about the price of silk. The dyeing has been very successful and the word has passed from mouth to mouth that our dyes are fast, consequently many people want us to dye their silk on a contract basis. I am extremely interested in this little job and hope it will go well.

I have had many invitations to go out and have had pleasant evenings with the Europeans in this place. Dining at the Residency is always fun but it does mean a mess jacket, but with a boy who puts in all the studs and waistcoat buttons it is not too bad.

I'm sure you must want to know what I do all day, so here is a general outline. Seven a.m., called with tea and fruit, have time to read a book before shaving and bathing for breakfast at 7.30. I always wear white shorts, open-necked shirt and long stockings when I am in the office. Breakfast begins with the news from London and we hear a commentary at 8.00 a.m. Work starts at 8.30 and I deal with files and the post when it arrives later. I am in the office until lunch at 1.00 p.m. I lie down after lunch until my Malay tutor arrives and my lesson lasts until 4.00 p.m. Then tea at 4.15 and then games until 7.00 p.m. when it gets dark. We then have a drink on the veranda with a standard electric light. I change and am in time for the news at 8.30 and then we have dinner. I am usually in bed by 10.00 p.m. I am feeling very fit and well except for some blasted things which have bitten my ankles and they take about a week to clear up. I don't think they are mosquitoes as we are not supposed to have any here, but whatever they are I do not like them.

I went on a river trip yesterday and had a very exciting time. I went with the Commissioner of Police in the police launch which has an outboard motor. We went fifteen miles up the river and saw places where tigers and other animals had come down to the bank to drink. The river is very wide but very shallow and we were nearly overturned four times when the boat hit a submerged tree trunk when travelling at speed. Whenever this happened the man standing in the bow, who was supposed to watch for these things, was thrown into the water; all the others in the crew rushed to one side to drag him out and only the fact that Leonard Knight, the Commissioner, is over sixteen stones saved us from capsizing. We started at nine and were back about seven; I was very tired, mostly nervous strain I think. The country is quite beautiful and it was very cool on the river in a covered launch.

Tomorrow the Residency party is going out to an island in the Government launch, we will start before breakfast and be back about five. The Muslim fasting month begins on Monday and we have a holiday on Tuesday because it is Trengganu National Day. I like the idea of having Mohammedan holidays, Chinese New Year, the odd Indian celebration and our own holidays. Tonight I am going out to dinner with the Engineer but hope to fit in a game of golf beforehand.

I must finish now as the Clipper is due out soon,

Your affectionate son.

Life in Trengganu went on at a leisurely and pleasant pace; it seemed a far cry from England and the rationing, etc., which the people at home were suffering. We listened to the news every day but never imagined the awful fate that was about to overtake us. Much of my time was spent liaising with the Forces in Kelantan to the north of us but, as far as I can remember, there was no plan for the evacuation of people in the event of an attack by the Japanese.

It's easy to understand why this was so. The British were in Malaya as protectors and advisers and it would have created, I am sure, alarm and distrust if there had been any known plan for the evacuation of the British while other nationalities were left to face the Japanese. We continued our exercises with the local defence force but these troops were no match for any invading Japanese force. I suppose we hoped an invasion would not happen and prayed that it should not. Certainly there was no hint of the impending catastrophe in my letters home. Letters from my father in Nigeria arrived in two weeks via South Africa, those from England took somewhat longer. I was at pains to keep both my parents up to date with what I was doing; sometimes this was difficult as I did not have all that amount of spare time to write letters. What would I not have done for a copying machine or a modern word processor!

I began to be well accepted by other members of the European community and received an increasing number of invitations to dinner and days out to the islands. At first I could not understand a certain reticence to welcome me with open arms – or the equivalent. In these small expatriate enclaves it is essential that everyone gets on with everyone else and that no friction or jealousies develop. I soon found that the Malayan Civil Services officers had a reputation for being somewhat stand-offish and were known as the 'heaven born'. Whether this was justified I do not know but it was understandable as all the most senior posts in the States and Districts were held by M.C.S. officers. I well remember a case after the War when, as a District Magistrate, I had to try a member of the planting community who had threatened one of his estate guards with a revolver. My task was made easier as the man was in no way a personal friend of mine.

My letters home reflected this increased social activity.

Kuala Trengganu
2nd October 1941

My dear Mum,

Thank you so much for the cable and the letter dated August 11th which arrived today. I can't understand why you have not had a Clipper mail because I posted one before I came up to Trengganu. There has been a little trouble and I am beginning to wonder whether it is worth while posting Clipper.

Your holiday seemed to be starting fairly well and I hope you enjoyed it. Transport must be very difficult with the absence of a good bus service and I sympathise with you having to walk such long distances.

Your garden does not appear to be going too well and I hope you managed to get it dug up and planted for the winter vegetables. [Home-grown vegetables became an increasingly important factor in every household as the War in Europe caused more and more belts to be tightened.] You will see a marked change in my diet when I come on leave. We have to get our meat and many other commodities from the Cold Storage in Kota Bharu which is 100 miles away and the return journey takes all day. Fish, however, is good and plentiful and we have at least one fish meal every day. Crab is good and an excellent dish which the cook manages to concoct is macaroni and crab pie. Vegetables are unusual onions, a red bean with sweet potatoes and tinned peas are those we see most often. I haven't seen a pineapple since I arrived but other fruit is plentiful – bananas, mangosteens, apples from Australia and rambutans are the most popular. I eat a lot of fruit because I have it with early morning tea, with breakfast and again at tea-time.

The main event these last few days has been the purchase of a car. I am now the proud owner of a 14/6 Wolseley with dual carburettors. I asked in the town one morning if anyone knew of a second-hand car for sale and a dealer turned up the next day to say that a Tengku (member of the Royal Family) wanted to sell his as he was buying a new car. I tried it and liked it and he finally accepted $1,500, which is dirt cheap as the equivalent model is $2,500 in Singapore. It is a 1940 model, white with blue seats and has a marvellous selection of gadgets. It has a fog lamp, spot lamp, twin horns, etc., etc. I am lucky to get it because cars are very scarce, a man came down from Kelantan with one like it but wanted and had been offered $2,500 on a trade-in. Since I am a Government servant I get a free driving licence and free road tax – which makes a difference. We need two cars here because when I am in the office with the B.A. Mrs. de Moubray can drive it. She is very generous and always puts in more petrol that she uses. The great advantage is that I can accept invitations without having to find someone to give me a lift or to ask for the use of the Residency car. I don't like doing that as the driver has to turn out and either wait for me or make a second journey to collect me. Mat, my boy, hasn't a lot to do so he polishes it every day and it looks great.

I have been playing quite a lot of golf lately and am glad to say that my eye seems to be in again; my tennis has also improved. Last night we had some tennis arranged but it started to drizzle so Mrs. De Moubray and I set out to play a few holes. I started 4,5,4,3,4,3 and then the rain started in earnest.

One evening last week I went shooting with Noel Rees, the Head of Education in the state. He is known as 'tinggi', which means tall, as he is well over six feet and considerably taller than the average Malay or Chinese. We didn't have much luck but we did get some pigeons. The country round here is absolutely stiff with tigers and there are some elephants. Knight, the Commissioner of Police, went after an elephant the other day but it had moved away and Knight did not have enough time to follow it up.

I have been out to dinner a lot lately. A sea captain who has been here for many years is leaving and everyone seems to be giving a party for him. I have been to many of them and have been having an excellent time.

I got your cable yesterday saying that you had got my letter dated September 4th. That is good news. If ever you have to cable again, I think 'Patterson, Kuala Trengganu' will find me as I am pretty well known around the town. It is a great relief to know that my letters are getting through and I will certainly write by American Clipper every time.

At the moment we have Lady Sansom staying at the Residency; she is a delightful and extremely interesting person. She has been all over the world and her husband is an acknowledged expert on Japanese affairs. She has come up to see the country and I have been taking her round in the car. We have been taking photographs and she has done a lot of sketching.

I'm afraid I must finish this now as it is mail day.

Love to all the family.

Life for me was fascinating and I hardly had time to think. I became a sort of Social Secretary as we had many visitors to the state, it was probably the most unspoiled part of Malaya. The beaches were spectacular and the people charming and interesting. Local crafts included silk weaving and the making of fine silver-ware. I also had my own schedule of work and this entailed visits to many parts of the state. Trengganu is long and narrow and in those days had one single track road running parallel with the coast; the numerous rivers were crossed by a human-powered ferry. All this has now been replaced by a modern highway and bridges.

I had a frightening experience when returning from one of my visits to the south. Just after it got dark (it gets dark every day of the year at about seven o'clock), I saw in my headlights a tiger and a tigress. As I accelerated so did they and as I slowed down they came closer and closer to the car. This continued for some miles and I just did not know what to do; I quickly checked that all the windows were closed, as we usually travelled with them wide open because of the heat. At last we arrived at a village and the tigers bounded off the road into the jungle. The villagers saw a very frightened European who had the greatest difficulty in telling them what had happened. One problem was that the Malays do not, because of superstition, refer to the tiger by the usual term of 'harimau'; they call him 'Dato Pa Bleng', 'The Honourable Grandfather of Stripes'.

On another occasion I visited a village where the headman showed me where they had built an enclosure for their cattle. It was about six feet high and quite robust but the tiger had jumped into the compound, killed one of their cattle, thrown it over his back and jumped out again. The strength of these magnificent animals is awesome.

My letters home were still full of all that I was doing and no reference to the impending gloom, even though it was a mere five or six weeks away.

Kuala Trengganu
1st November 1941

My dear Mum,

No letter has arrived from you for some time but I hope I will receive one before this letter is finished. I see that a Clipper is due on November 3rd and will probably leave about 7th.

The B.A. and Mrs. de Moubray have been away on local leave for nearly two weeks and will be returning tomorrow. Things have gone pretty smoothly and the visit of the Rt. Rev. Lord Bishop of Singapore went off with little trouble. I enjoyed it very much and you will see why in a moment. He arrived on the 28th in time for lunch and we had that in Cobden-Ramsay's house as he is acting for the B.A. while he is away. The Bishop was in good form and we had a most enjoyable meal. Afterwards we came back here to get things organised for the evening service. We had to arrange for copies of the hymn sheets as we did not have enough hymn books. When all this was fixed we had tea in the garden and he asked me about my family; when I told him about Dad in Nigeria he asked if I knew E. K. Featherstone. He said that they had served in the Army together and had spent many leaves in each other's company. It transpired that the Bishop, Leonard Wilson, and his two younger brothers had been at my old school and knew some of the masters who were there in my day. We had a long discussion and it was not surprising that the baptism was five minutes late.

We had evensong with sermon at 7.00 p.m., followed by a dinner party for twelve. The cook managed to produce a very respectable meal after I had discussed the proposed menu with him. Earlier in the day the Bishop asked if it would be possible to have a game of bridge but with the dinner party that seemed unlikely. Since Cobden-Ramsay is not married Mrs. Knight took the head of the table; I had tipped her off about the bridge and with great tact she brought the proceedings to a close at 9.45 p.m. and we got down to the cards. Knight and I played against the Bishop and Cobden-Ramsay and the Bishop turned out to be a very fine player. It was pretty even until the Bishop bid and made a grand slam; that settled things as far as we were concerned and we were lucky to get away losing only one dollar. When he left the Bishop said that if I ever thought of getting married and he was in the country he would be delighted to perform the ceremony.

2nd November

The B.A. returns today and I must finish this letter and then sort out all the papers which need his immediate attention. I think everything is in order and I hope he is not displeased with the way things have been run while he has been away.

My car has been a disaster as the previous owner saved money by running it without the proper level of oil. It suddenly developed the most horrendous engine noise and the power unit had to be sent to Singapore for a complete rebuild. After a lot of pressure from me, the previous owner and his agent are meeting the cost of the repairs which will be about what I paid for the machine.

I will be very glad to see the car back again as the Residency car is away and the rains are beginning. Last night we had a most frightening thunderstorm, one flash of lightning was so close that you could hear the crackle of the electricity as it hit the earth. It made the wireless impossible and we missed the news from London, which is most unusual. The wind came up very quickly and the six house-boys who usually loaf around the place were suddenly charged with dynamic energy and rushed around closing all the windows and shutters. It must be the beginning of the monsoon as it has not stopped raining all day.

My Malay teacher is due in a moment so I must stop now.
Love to all the family.

Things went on pretty much as usual and my letters home were full of comments on the family, particularly my young brother who had just been made a prefect and Captain of the 2nd XV. I was working pretty hard and had been introduced to the mysteries of Government Estimates. An added complication in Trengganu was that they were prepared in the Arabic script and then translated into English; it really was a laborious task.

As late as the beginning of December 1941 I was writing home saying that Mrs. Knight was going to give me two puppies, the result of their dachshund chasing a Sealyham bitch. I spent many evenings out shooting and got a lot of tennis and golf. The war seemed very far away, even though we listened every morning and evening to the progress of the campaign in North Africa.

To this day, I remember many things about my time in Trengganu. The dining table in the Residency was surrounded by a low wooden wall and behind this sat a small boy who pulled the 'punka'. This was a piece of material, attached to a pole, and suspended from the ceiling. The boy pulled it backwards and forwards to create a cooling draught over the table. He found he could do that by tying the string to his toe and moving his foot up and down. As the meal progressed, the punka got slower and slower until the B.A. called for a glass of cold water. The boy woke up with a start when it was poured over him and the punka leaped into agitated action.

There were so many things happening that I had difficulty in giving my parents a full picture of my life; some were amusing and at least one, apart from the tigers, quite frightening.

One day we had a member of the planting community to stay and he asked me, 'What is the rig for dinner this evening?' I told him it was black tie, dinner or mess jacket, or he could wear Malay dress baju (shirt), seluar (trousers) and a sarong.

George de Moubray was everyone's idea of a senior Colonial Civil Servant. He was tall, always immaculately dressed and a brilliant linguist. He set great store on punctuality and it was more than my career was worth to be late for dinner. The meal every evening was a ritual; the B.A. sat at one end of the table and Mrs. de Moubray at the other. It was served by four house boys in white uniforms and black songkoks, the Malay head-dress.

Imagine my horror when our guest appeared for dinner in a shirt and sarong which were obviously his sleeping attire. I cannot remember how we got through the evening but I do recall it was a pretty sticky session.

I lived in a small bungalow in the grounds of the Residency and one evening as I set out to walk the thirty yards or so for dinner, I saw, in the middle of the path, a king cobra. I have always been absolutely terrified of snakes and it was all I could do to retreat and find my shot gun. I blasted its head off and called my boy to carry away the carcass. That was bad enough but Mat said to me, 'You must take care, Tuan, because the snake's mate will come looking for it.' You can imagine my terror when, during the night, I heard a scratching noise on the walls of the bungalow. It turned out to be a cow which had escaped and strayed into the Residency grounds. Indeed, the cobra came looking for its mate and I shot it three days later; only then could I sleep at night. To this day the sight of a snake, even behind glass in a zoo, sends shivers down my spine.

Chapter 3

Escape from Trengganu

And then it happened. Japanese ships had been sighted making towards the coast of Kelantan, the state immediately north of Trengganu, on 7th December. Our aircraft had difficulty identifying the ships because of the very bad weather. It had been assumed that the Japanese were unlikely to mount an invasion of Malaya from the sea until the end of the monsoon season. Shortly after midnight 7th-8th December, the Japanese landed on the beaches not far from Kota Bharu town. It would appear that they made such a successful approach because they were guided by lights displayed prominently on high ground behind the beaches.

The Japanese met stiff resistance but the defence line was thin and the Japanese soon captured the airfield that the troops were protecting. We heard of all of this by telephone and our main task was to round up the Japanese in Trengganu. There was a large contingent of them at Dungun at a mine called Bukit Besi – Malay for 'The Hill of Iron'. They had been working for years at this mine and were very upset when taken into custody.

By 10th December the Japanese had advanced so far that the route out of the state northwards was impossible; we then received the disturbing news – subsequently proved to be incorrect – that the Japanese had landed at Kuantan. This town lies on the coast of Pahang, immediately south of Trengganu; transports had indeed been sighted and this led to the *Prince of Wales* and *Repulse* being ordered to sail from Singapore. We were forced to the conclusion that we were cut off and the only escape was overland, trying to reach Kuala Lipis. After weighing all the odds, the British Adviser decided that we should attempt this journey even though it had been done by only three Europeans previously, and then in dry weather; in our case it rained most days.

A total of seventeen people, accompanied by three Malay guides, made the journey. Not much could be planned and we could only carry food and small valuables. I can remember well the sadness of having to say good-bye to my boy Mat and to leave my car with the engine running – once again without oil – so that it would be of no use to the Japanese.

We started from a place called Jerangau, forty miles from Kuala Trengganu, and it took us five hours to cover that distance by car as the roads were so bad. There we divided the party into three groups. It was decided that I should lead the first group and make as much speed as possible, hoping to arrange for motor boats to go up the Tembeling river to meet the people following behind. In the second group were the three ladies, Mrs. Knight, Dr. Cecily Williams and the wife of a member of the Volunteers who had already been called up. Mrs. Knight looked as elegant as she always did but I recall that her footwear was hardly designed for jungle trekking. This group was to move as fast as the ladies could manage and the third was to follow in easy stages.

The range of mountains which runs down the centre of Malaya, rather like a spine, rises to 3,000 feet. Even though it is so close to the equator, it is extremely cold at night and we only had the clothes for walking in the heat of the day. Without our Malay guides we would not have been able to do the journey; they had a remarkable sense of direction taking us up river beds and over tracks that were almost invisible to us. The going was never easy, sometimes downright frightening when one had to cross a raging torrent on a bridge that consisted of one slippery tree trunk.

On the first day as we climbed away from the coast we were suddenly aware of aircraft circling over our heads. The jungle is thick and it was some time before we managed to get to a clearing on a hillside and then we saw a most incredible sight. Over us circled Japanese torpedo bombers, flying slowly at little more than tree-top height and there, out at sea, were the huge battleships *Prince of Wales* and *Repulse* and their escorting de-stroyers. We did not see the attack on these magnificent ships, which started at about 11.00 a.m., and such was the devastating effect of the torpedo and high level bombing that the ships went down by 1.30 p.m. Two thousand one hundred and eighty-five of the ships' crew were saved but the loss of two battleships had a significant impact on morale. Only a week previously their arrival in Singapore had been an occasion of great rejoicing and suddenly they were no more. Much has been written about the campaign in Malaya and it is not my intention to add more than a personal view but, having seen something of the R.A.F. and its exploits in this country, it did seem that Malaya was provided with very few modern aircraft.

Our journey across the country was difficult in the extreme and it was marvellous to see the courage of the ladies in the next group. We had to wade through rivers and streams and the dank jungle is a hiding place for leeches. At regular intervals we had to stop, remove all of our clothes and burn off those awful creatures with a lighted cigarette. They get into the most private places, sinking their sharp fangs below the skin and sucking blood; when sated they will drop off but to pull them off will leave a wound which will almost certainly go septic. These things come in all sizes, from the tiddlers about half an inch long to huge monsters of three inches and more. They are without doubt one of the nastiest animals I have ever encountered.

Food was very simple. Our guide carried a cast iron cooking pot and morning and evening he cooked rice, which we ate with salt and a little fish or meat. It was a foretaste of the diet which I was to have for three and a half years as a 'guest' of the Japanese. Our guide seemed fit enough on it, he was agile and never seemed to tire, but by the end of the day the rest of us were absolutely exhausted.

Mosquitoes were another problem but we had packed nets in our little sacks and put these over our faces at night. We usually slept on a sand-bank in a river as the guide said that was the safest place. Fires were lit at each end of our camp to keep us warm and to deter wild animals such as tigers.

Sleep was difficult but we usually managed a few hours before the dawn woke us. I remember one night when I heard a coughing noise and thought that one of my companions must have caught a cold – quite possible as we were wet through most of the day. I could not see much by the light of the fire's last embers; next morning our guide, with teeth chattering, pointed out the pug marks of a tiger which had circled our fires two or three times. I had a pair of Smith and Wesson revolvers but I don't think they would have been much use.

After the third day, the going got a little easier as it was mainly down-hill. On one occasion we saw a wonderful sight as a herd of elephants made their way down the hill-side on the opposite side of the valley. The leading group cleared a path by pulling up the trees and tossing them over their shoulders. We watched, absolutely fascinated, and were amazed at the speed they managed to achieve. It was all done so quietly, the only noise being the snap of the branches and the rustle of the leaves.

On the sixth day we arrived at the upper reaches of the Tembeling River. At that point it is not very wide but very fast-flowing and there are numerous rapids. Our guides set about making rafts and it was amazing to see how quickly they managed to make a craft that took three people. The Malay weapons are the kris, a sort of dagger, and the parang, which is not unlike the Gurkha kukri. The parang is straight, about eighteen inches long with a wooden handle and sharpened on one side of the blade. Bamboos, about fifteen feet long, were cut down from the clumps which grew on the river banks. Some were trimmed to form the platform of the raft and the bark was stripped from others and used to bind the platform together. When finished, the raft was about twelve feet long and four feet wide with three layers of bamboos; the guides steered the craft with more bamboo poles.

It really was a hair-raising journey down the river and its rapids; the raft was awash most of the time and we were soaked throughout the journey. If it had not been so serious an expedition, it would have been quite fun. We made very good time and once we got to the broader parts of the river, after all the rapids, we were met by two motor boats which had been sent to meet us by the Resident of Pahang. In one of the boats was the Forestry Officer from Trengganu who had been based in the south of the state near Kemaman and knew that the reports of a landing at Kuantan were false. How glad we were to see the rescue party; we had one tin of corned beef left but plenty of rice and salt.

Where the river comes close to the railway we left the boats and flagged down a freight train at Tembeling Halt to take us to the state capital of Kuala Lipis. I remember being absolutely furious when we were made to pay third class fares for our ride on the freight train.

The other two parties arrived safely and I was amazed to see how well the three ladies had stood up to the journey. It was, I suppose, a pretty fine achievement but there was a marked feeling of anticlimax because it was so unnecessary. Had the intelligence from Kuantan been correct about the fact that there was no Japanese landing on the beaches, we could have motored out with at least some of our belongings.

On the 18th I sent my father a cable, which he did not receive until the 27th, which read, 'Safe, proceeding Singapore, will wire later.'

I managed to scrounge a few clothes in Kuala Lipis and set out for Singapore to report back to the Army as it was clear that there was no further job for me in the civil administration. There were quite a few people in my situation; I held the King's Commission but had no regiment for pay and rations. The dilemma was summed up in a letter I wrote home soon after Christmas.

c/o Malayan Establishment Office,
Singapore.
26th December 1941

My dear Mum,

I am afraid that this letter can bring you nothing but depressing news, the only good news being that I am safe and well. I hardly know where to start because I have so much to tell you. An awful lot of the most recent part of my experiences must remain untold but I shall have a lot to tell you when we meet again after all this turmoil.

I am now back in the Army with my old rank and am waiting for somewhere to go. I have no regular unit in this country so will have to wait until they decide where they are going to send me. At the moment I am in a camp on Singapore Island with a lot of officers in my position. What they are going to do with us I do not know but I shall probably be attached to some unit or battery out here.

The worst news of all is that I have lost absolutely everything in this country and there is little chance of getting anything back. We were cut off and all the Europeans came out through the jungle. Three of us went ahead carrying what we could with the help of a few local carriers. We were seven days in the jungle before we met a party coming up to meet us in motor boats. Really it was quite fun, eating off banana leaves and living on rice and the little tinned food we managed to carry. When we were met we had one tin of corned beef left but plenty of rice. I was very sad to leave all my beautiful things behind but many other people have had similar bad luck. To have two people in the family have the same experience within such a short space of time must, I think, indicate some great wrong done by our ancestors in the past. [A reference to the fact my Uncle Fred and his wife escaped from France in front of the German advance but lost everything in the panic.]

When I arrived in Singapore to report as instructed, I stayed with Guy Machado, who is a Eurasian school-master who was working with us. They have a queer household and had just moved into a new house so we had to sleep on the floor. The next day I had the good luck to meet Lady Sanson, who stayed with us some time ago. She asked me if I would like to go and stay with them. An offer which I accepted with alacrity. Her husband Sir George Sanson is a Far Eastern expert who was in our embassy in Tokyo for a long time. He is a most charming man and I had a marvellous time with them, they were most kind and the rest and conversation with them was the best tonic I could have had. They have two cars (mine, of course, has gone) and they kindly lent me one when I wanted to do anything. I managed to collect a few clothes in which to exist and any I did not have Sir George lent me. I can't tell you how marvellous they were to me; Lady Sanson is absolutely charming and took me to lunch and to swim at the Tanglin Club. This is the exclusive club out here; everybody who is anybody is a member. The membership is above my salary level but sometime when I rise in the service I will join. We had a marvellous Christmas lunch with an Australian journalist, who seems to spend much of his time running up and down the Burma Road in lorries. A great man who cares nothing for anybody and in consequence is a joy to talk to.

When I went to stay with Lady Sanson she had two charming girls with her. One, an American, is secretary to one of the big noises out here and the other is married to one of the members of our Embassy in Chunking; she hopes to go there soon. Of course, I fell for the American and took her out to dinner and a show, which was most enjoyable. Apparently she married a waster in America and then divorced him, coming out soon after to do her bit. The infatuation passed quickly and I am once again with my head above water.

When I arrived here I was told by the Establishment Office that I was released for military service as I held the King's Commission and, anyway, there was no job for me. Now nobody knows what to do with me and I am hanging about all day. My army pay is being made up to my civil pay, which is nearly twice as much. It will take some saving to replace all that I have lost but, as I said before, many other people are in the same situation.

I've had no news from you for a long time but I did have a note and a present from Aunt Doris and a card from Donald and Ian. Please thank them, it was the only reminder of Christmas I had. I can't write to them at the moment but I will do so when I can.

I had a letter from Dad written at the end of November, exhorting me to be careful with money and to get through my exams quickly. Who cares about these things now? They can wait.

We've got to drive these yellow swine out of here before there is
any talk of exams. My Malay is now pretty good and I can always
get a taxi while other people are blundering around in the dark.

You will be interested to hear that the only thing of any value I
have left is a rather fine moustache; it is a good disguise and even
my friends fail to recognise me. I saw the B.A. the other day and
he looked twice. He is in an awful state and I am very sorry for
him. I expect he will retire now because he was fairly near and is
so senior he just can't be thrown into any job.

I'm afraid this must be a very disappointing letter for you to
receive but I am doing what I can to keep happy and to forget all
that has passed. I will let you have news as often as I can.
                        Always your loving son.

That letter was the last that I would be able to write to either of my
parents. Things happened rapidly in Singapore and Malaya but there was
an air of unreality which, I am sure, made people almost punch-drunk. In
quick succession the Europeans were evacuated from Penang, the *Prince
of Wales* and the *Repulse* were sunk and the advance of the Japanese down
the peninsula was quick and seemed to be unstoppable. Optimism that
Singapore was a fortress was quickly, in my case, replaced with a realisa-
tion that disaster was just around the corner.

Chapter 4

The Fall of Singapore

After a few days of wondering what I would do, I was told to report to the 3rd Anti-Aircraft Regiment. As a field gunner I found this a little confusing but Colonel Hugonin – a first class wicket-keeper for the Army cricket team – encouragingly said that it would not be too difficult for me to get the hang of things; they fired vertically while we shot horizontally. Fortunately I was never called upon to command an anti-aircraft gun in action as I was posted to a liaison role with the R.A.F.

We sat in a command post trying to anticipate the next Japanese air attack. By the time I arrived on the scene most of our airfields had been knocked out of action and the Japanese had unchallenged air supremacy. The few aircraft that were still operational were no match for the Japanese bombers and their escorting fighters. I believe we did have a few Spitfires but they were still in packing cases and the Brewster Buffaloes were no match for the Japanese Zeros. There was a universal belief that the Japanese pilots would black out in tight turns. I had proof that this was rubbish as I flew in a bomber looking at our camouflage and a Zero performed acrobatic loops round our plane. We landed at great speed.

The role of the R.A.F. liaison officer soon became redundant and I was ordered to Fort Canning as a Staff Officer 'A' on Brigadier Newbiggin's staff. Soon after this I was promoted Captain, an event which took some time to filter through the system but it did have the local effect of increasing my pay. My portfolio was wide-ranging, varying from the writing of citations for honours in the field to authorising the replacement of vehicles lost. I can remember to this day an Australian Colonel, who stormed into my office and used a number of words which I did not understand, questioning the need for him to sign a quote '—!!ing' form in order to get a replacement for the jeep that had been blown up under him. I was particularly delighted to see that a citation I drafted for a D.S.O. for an Australian Brigadier Blackburn passed upwards through the system and he was awarded a V.C.

By this time I had gone to live with a Major Andrews in comfortable married quarters. But, there was still this difficulty of accepting the inevitable. He had two of the most beautiful springer spaniels and one of my tasks was to shoot these beautiful animals in order to prevent them from falling into enemy hands. I felt sick as I threw them down a convenient bore hole.

My work as a liaison officer with the R.A.F. was on a shift basis and when I was not working I spent much of my time at the Swimming Club. Life seemed to go on much as usual, even though Singapore was being bombed almost hourly. There was dancing in the evening in Raffles and at all the other clubs in Singapore. Whether it was a desire to keep a stiff upper lip or an inability to face facts one will never know.

I was only twenty-one years of age and the events in Singapore made a lasting impression on me. The bombings of the civilian population caused immense damage and casualties; wherever one went the emergency services were trying to cope with the dead and dying on the streets.

On 1st January 1942 I started my diary, which was to prove the inspiration for this book and the source of a lot of the facts which have jolted my memories even after all these years. It is a Charles Lett's pocket diary measuring 2" x 4" and into it I managed to get about two and a half years of notes. The Japanese were very hard on people who kept diaries, and to this day I do not remember how I concealed it or how I transported it from camp to camp as I made the Japanese Cook's Tour from Singapore to Mukden in Manchuria.

The diary confirms that I reported to 'A' branch on 11th January and was told that I was to be promoted Captain from that date. I had difficulty in getting somewhere to lay my head and, once again, Lady Sanson came to the rescue and I spent a couple of days with her before moving into a quarter with Major Andrews.

I spent the rest of January in Fort Canning, the administrative headquarters of the Army in Singapore. It was a large fortress-type complex and it took me days to find my way around. All the time the Japanese were advancing towards Singapore, our air defences were non-existent and the bombers came over once or twice a day without any opposition. On 1st February the Argyll and Sutherland Highlanders marched across the Causeway with pipes playing and colours flying in a defiant gesture before the Causeway was blown up. It didn't take the Japanese all that long to repair it.

Two days previously four large liners, two British and two American, had brought the troops of the Eighteenth Division – all to be captured before they had time to acclimatise themselves. I was sent to one of the American ships with confidential documents and the scenes at the docks were an absolute shambles. Already troops, particularly from some of the Australian forces, were trying to get to the ships in front of the women and children whose evacuation had now been ordered. The Japanese bombers were causing death and destruction on a vast scale and most of the dockside labourers had already decided that they had had enough. On the way to the docks I got caught in an air raid, flung myself into a ditch but not soon enough to prevent damage to my left ear, which is still much less efficient than the right one. On board the Captain took the documents to his safe and then asked me whether it would not be a bad thing if I was in his cabin when they sailed. I was sorely tempted but went back to my desk.

On 7th February I went to see Mrs. de Moubray and learned that the B.A. had been attached to one of the Australian formations and had been wounded on the Bukit Timah road. I heard that one of the police cadets who had come out on the ship with me had been killed with an Army unit he had joined.

By 10th February I had moved into Fort Canning and was sleeping on a mattress on the office floor. The bombing was unrelenting and we were subjected to the additional hazard of shells from the Japanese artillery which was now well within range. I nearly met my end when a shell landed very close to us when I was in Union Building. I noted that I had been promoted Captain with effect from 12th January but 'do not see much chance of drawing back pay'.

Late in the afternoon of 11th February a sergeant came into my office, saluted and said, 'General Percival would like to see you, Sir.' I realised that things had reached a pretty desperate state but hoped the blame would not be attached to me. I grabbed my cap and followed the sergeant to the General's office. I saluted and the General said, 'Do come and sit down, I want a word or two with you.' I really did not know what was to come as I had no inkling that the great man even knew of my existence – a very junior officer on his staff. 'I understand,' he said, 'that you speak the language of the country pretty well and that you have a reputation for driving cars very quickly and very safely. My A.D.C. has been given permission to leave Singapore. Would you like to take his place and look after me?' When I said that I would like the job, the General added, 'That is fine but you realise how serious is the situation we are facing and you may well become a prisoner of the Japanese.' In my own mind I had already faced up to that distasteful conclusion because it seemed that Singapore could not last out more than a few days. I moved into an adjoining office and got very little sleep that first night as messages came flooding in from all points of the compass.

The next day was spent in Battle Headquarters as I familiarised myself with the geography and the personalities. Up till then the only senior officer I had met more than once was my own Brigadier Newbiggin, the head of 'A' Branch. Conferences were being held almost hourly as the seriousness of Singapore's plight developed. That afternoon I drove the General to Government House to see the Governor Sir Shenton Thomas who was, of course, Governor and Commander-in-Chief. He recognised me and asked how I was liking my new job, saying that it must have been a great change from the peace and tranquillity of Trengganu.

On 13th February I drove the General round all the formations in Singapore. By that time the Japanese had pushed our forces back and we were hemmed into a very small area. We were already drawing water from behind the Japanese lines, as they had advanced beyond the MacRitchie reservoirs but had not cut off the supplies. The skies were full of Japanese planes and on two occasions we were machine-gunned from the air – an extremely unpleasant experience. I was surprised to see, when I caught a quick glance in my rear mirror, that the General was having a well-earned nap.

On that day I learned that two young officers, who had become good friends of mine, had been killed by a shell in Fort Canning. It suddenly brought home to me the horror and futility of war.

On 14th February we slept in the 'Battle Box' and the shelling and bombing was unrelenting. We saw His Excellency the Governor once more and I believe that this was the moment when it was finally decided that Singapore could not hold out any longer, and that we would have to surrender on the best terms we could negotiate. Government House was a prime target for the bombers but Lady Thomas, who was quite ill at the time, had made a bed under the billiard table. I tried to send a message to my mother but clearly it did not get through – or if it did, there is no record of it. My diary contains the entry, 'Shell lifted the car off the road today but little damage done.' Really, how laid back can you get?

Perhaps the most fateful day of my whole life was Sunday 15th February 1942 – Black Sunday. It started with a Communion Service in Fort Canning and then the bad news never stopped. The General told me to go to the Headquarters of the Australian Forces, see Maj.-Gen. Gordon

Bennett and tell him that it was our intention to meet the Japanese later that day and surrender on as good terms as we could negotiate. When I arrived at the Australian Headquarters Gordon Bennett was not to be seen and I was told that any messages I had could be handed over to Brig. (later Maj.-Gen.) Callaghan, he was accompanied by his senior staff officers, Col. Thyer and Col. Kent-Hughes. Some years later I saw Col. Kent-Hughes when he visited Malaya as leader of the Opposition in the Victorian Parliament. I did not discover what had happened to Gordon Bennett, but subsequently it seems clear that he left Singapore with his A.D.C. Captain Walker and a staff major before the surrender.

Late in the afternoon the word came that a party was to drive out to Bukit Timah Road to meet the Japanese Commander. Brigadier Torrance the chief of the General Staff had already made contact with the Japanese with a Major Wilde who was a fluent Japanese speaker. We set out in two cars, Brigadiers Torrance and Newbiggin with Major Wilde in the first car, and General Percival with a sergeant carrying a white flag and me driving the second car. We were stopped at the junction of Bukit Timah and Adam Road by a Japanese tank and the General was escorted to the Ford Factory to meet General Yamashita. General Percival was not able to

General Percival surrenders to the Japanese, 15th February, 1942.

The surrender of Singapore at 7 p.m., 15th February, 1942. Lieut. General Yamashita and General Percival at the interview.

secure many concessions, except that the front-line Japanese fighting troops were to be kept out of Singapore. Little did he imagine that some years later he would be present at Yamashita's capitulation.

I spent a very uncomfortable three hours staring down the gun barrel of the Japanese tank, hoping against hope that our troops would have the good sense not to open fire. Things were so confused by that time that anything could happen. Eventually a very dejected British party arrived back and we returned to Fort Canning in the knowledge that our surrender at 8.30 p.m. was, to all intents and purposes, unconditional.

On the way back to Fort Canning we called at Government House so that the General could tell the Governor, Sir Shenton Thomas, about his meeting with Yamashita. His Excellency greeted us with a very welcome whisky and soda but it was a sad occasion for the Commander-in-Chief of one of the jewels in the Empire. Lady Thomas, I remember, was remarkably cheerful and understanding, although not at all well at the time.

Chapter 5

Personal Views

I suppose this is the best place in this book to express some of my thoughts about the battle in Malaya and the fall of Singapore. Whenever I have mentioned my part in these proceedings, I have been asked a number of questions: what about the whisky-swilling planters? Would it not have been very different if the guns had pointed the right way? Why was everyone still dancing at Raffles when the Japanese were half way down the peninsula, and what sort of a man was Percival?

I have always had a great respect for the planting community, particularly for the way they stood fast in the face of attacks by the Communist terrorists after the war. Until I went to Malaya I had little idea how rubber moved from a tree to a tyre with Goodyear or Firestone imprinted on it. The planter's day starts before dawn, when the Indian or Chinese tappers leave their lines and go out to tap the rubber trees. They make a slanting cut round the tree, fix a metal spout at the base of the cut and under the spout attach a small ceramic bowl. Soon the milky white latex starts to flow and this must be collected before the heat of the day, when it starts to coagulate and can no longer be processed. This takes place during the afternoon so the planter works a pretty long day.

The mistake, I believe, was to try to form these valuable men – together with many others – into Volunteer Units with the idea that they would be fighting units. They did not have the time to train to be fighting units and could have played a much more important role as guides and interpreters. Many of the units arriving in Malaya would have been delighted to have experienced advisers, who could tell them the difference between a Chinese and a Japanese and who were fluent in the local languages. While the Malay Regiment battalions acquitted themselves well, the Volunteers were taken from important civil tasks to be a less than effective fighting unit. The majority of them were taken prisoner as 'other ranks' and not accorded officer status – not that it made a lot of difference to the Japanese.

People in Singapore were shocked when the first bombs fell and their reaction was to try to continue with life as before. Singapore was really a garrison town and not a fortress. The troops believed they were there to defend the Naval Base but the administrative troops were almost as numerous as the combat units. Many of the army personnel had their wives and families with them and, in such circumstances, it is difficult to concentrate on fighting the enemy rather than getting the family to safety. Even I entered a plaintive note in my diary: 'the feminine company was sadly lacking.' All my training as a gunnery officer was in isolated surroundings, where one did not have to think about the possibility of a shell falling short or going off course and killing ten or twenty Chinese. Such was the state of affairs during the last days of Singapore that, unlike the desert, no front line could be determined with any degree of certainty.

And now to the vexed question of the guns. The main purpose of these guns was to protect the Naval Base from attack from the sea and so they were sited. These guns were fortress artillery, huge static weapons that took an age to load and fire. The shells were 15" in diameter, weighed half a ton and were armour-piercing, specially designed to inflict maximum damage on ships particularly warships. The shells would have been quite useless against Japanese infantry crawling through the jungles of Johore. Had the guns been able to fire into Johore they would have been sited over the Palace of the Sultan, a loyal subject who, I believe, had already given enough money from his own personal fortune to buy two or three Spitfires for the R.A.F.!

What sort of a man was General Percival? Physically he was unimpressive. Tall and thin, the shorts we had to wear did not suit him at all and made his legs look even thinner than they were. He walked with a slight stoop and had a habit of inclining his head when he was listening to you. His teeth protruded slightly and this gave him a very slight lisp when he spoke; he always listened attentively and spoke quietly, with none of the shouting and bombast one sometimes associates with senior officers.

He was a devout, committed Christian and attended Communion every Sunday throughout his captivity so long as he was able. He set an example to everyone. He was always concerned about the troops, even though he was never really at ease talking to them. During the time I was with him in captivity in Singapore, the effect that the loss of the island had had on him was clear. He spent hours walking by himself, lost in reflecting on what might have been. He was a very fair man and in his book he accepted that the war materials had to go to Russia and the Middle East – even if it did mean that Malaya got nothing. He had been Chief of the General Staff of Malaya Command in 1936 and was amazed to see how little interest was then being shown in the defence of Singapore. Little seemed to have been done when he returned as G.O.C. in May 1941; he often referred to those wasted years when we discussed the harrowing events that had overtaken us.

It was typical of the General that when he left the Army, he worked without stint for the Red Cross and became, I believe, our national President. He was always kind and considerate to junior officers like me and, in my case, he was a shield from the criticism of very senior officers in the mess that I had to run during the first six months of our captivity. I admired him without reservation.

Fifty years after the event, the row which centres on the performance of the Australian troops has resurfaced. Documents which might have been released after thirty years were embargoed for a further twenty in order to save an embarrassing situation developing between the two Governments. The Prime Minister of Australia had already cast a pretty large stone into the pool by accusing Britain of sacrificing Singapore and putting Australia at risk.

I can only add fuel to this fire by reporting my own personal observations and experiences. There is no doubt that some of the Australians fought courageously and the exploits of No. 1 Squadron R.A.A.F. in the first few days of the war, when the Japanese were invading Kelantan, were outstanding. Three of the officers of that squadron, Flight Lieutenants 'Spud' Spurgeon, Sydney Downer and Ossie Diamond, were my squad companions for much of my time as a prisoner. One could not have wished for finer friends.

When I went down to the Docks at the end of January to deliver the confidential documents to the Captain of the American ship, all was chaos and confusion. By that time it had dawned on most people that Singapore's days were numbered and those who did not have to stay were making strenuous efforts to leave. Boarding permits had been issued to women and children but the dockside was a milling throng, fighting to get on the ships. From my personal observation, the vast majority of the troops were Australians who should still have been in the front line. I remember threatening one with my revolver as he stood between me and the gang-plank. The majority were very drunk on liquor they had looted from shops and bars as they streamed through Singapore. It was a dangerous situation, as the troops were in a fair state of panic and very trigger-happy. All the time waves of Japanese bombers were coming over the city, with the harbour and the big ships their main targets.

Undoubtedly some of the Australians fought well but one always felt that a lot of their formations were trading on the reputations deservedly gained by their fathers in the First World War. Whether it was true or not, rumour had it that many of their reinforcements had secured early release from prison by agreeing to join the Australian 8th Division.

Chapter 6

Into Captivity

Singapore surrendered on 15th February and on the morning of the 16th the first Japanese officers arrived at Fort Canning headquarters. All our small arms and other weapons were gathered together and made quite an impressive pile. It soon became clear that the Japanese had, at that time, no clear view of what they were going to do with the vast number of prisoners of war. No administrative troops appeared for some weeks and it appeared that we were going to be allowed to stay put for some time. However, on the morning of the 17th, orders were given that everyone had to march to Changi Camp on the eastern extremity of the island. This was a small area and nowhere near large enough for the troops that were supposed to go there. General Percival protested to the Japanese but, as usual on such occasions, his protests were to no avail. I still had the General's car and managed to take him out to Changi on one trip and I then returned to collect as much stuff as I could.

Never having been a prisoner before, it was difficult to know just what to take. I managed to find a certain amount of liquor – vast quantities had been destroyed in order to prevent it falling into the hands of the front line Japanese troops – and also such luxuries as razor blades and sewing needles.

The house which we were allocated in Changi had been a married officer's quarter and into it we were to fit General Percival, seven Brigadiers, one full Colonel, the General's batman, a sergeant cook and me. When we arrived troops had taken over the ground floor and it was not until the following day that we managed to move them to other accommodation. It was a tight fit but I was quite amazed to see how these very senior officers adapted to a very changed life style. Having had their every want looked after, they suddenly had to do most things for themselves –

41

such as laundry. For the first few weeks we existed on British Army rations and came to a quick conclusion that two meals a day was as much as they would cover.

The troops were organised in their various commands and the General set out to visit as many as possible. We still had the car but it was clear that that perk was not going to last for long. Everywhere we went people pressed upon us the odd luxury and we made it a rule that everything should be shared and handed into the central store which was under my control. This worked very well until the Colonel caught a fish and insisted on cooking and eating it himself – holding that the sharing rule applied only to tins and dry goods. I suppose the thing the senior officers missed most was their gin and tonic at lunch and one or more whiskies in the evening. I measured the daily ration and everyone made it last as long as possible in the evening but it did not last long. The house was on a hill overlooking the Straits of Johore and in normal circumstances it would have been ideal.

One afternoon we were treated to the impressive and frightening sight of units of the Japanese Navy steaming into the Singapore Naval Base. The straits are not very wide at that point and we had an excellent view of the huge ships and their crews lining the decks. At that time they were literally and metaphorically speaking on the crest of a wave. They had conquered all they had set out to achieve and had suffered no reverses; their success was reflected in our treatment.

When we became prisoners of war some of us believed that the behaviour of our captors would be governed by the terms of the international conventions covering the treatment of P.O.W.s: how wrong we were. There were two conventions which governed the treatment of the prisoners of war, the Hague Convention of 1907 and the Geneva Convention of 1929. Japan was a signatory of the first but, although her representative had signed the second, it was never ratified. The Japanese professed to follow the provisions of the Hague convention but denied that they were bound, in any way, by the Geneva agreement. This, of course, was much more far reaching than the former. We found ourselves dealing with fanatical and unpredictable people, liable to blow up at the slightest provocation – sometimes with no provocation at all. Throughout my captivity everything possible was done by the Japanese to humiliate and denigrate the officers, whenever they could in front of our troops. I believe this had the opposite effect to that which was intended, as our other ranks did not enjoy seeing their officers beaten by these loathsome little men.

The first few weeks in Changi we did not have much contact with the Japanese and the administration and rations were in the hands of our own senior officers. On 25th February I noted in my diary that we were all paraded in front of General Yamashita and that, having shaken hands with General Percival, he shook hands with me. Not an event I remember with any degree of satisfaction.

Boredom was one of the greatest problems we faced – apart from not knowing what the future held for us. We soon had classes organised in all sorts of subjects and started to cultivate any spare bit of ground in order to get fresh vegetables. I managed to buy some ducklings and guarded them carefully until they started to lay. Our rations got steadily shorter and at the end of February we had our first issue of rice, the commodity which was to be the basis of our diet for the next three and a half years. Our cook tried all different sorts of recipes in order to make it more interesting but we soon came to the conclusion that it was better to cook the rice in plain salted water and then add whatever one had in a tin to it.

We were allowed to swim in the sea and this was a great joy in the hot humid climate of Singapore. By the end of the first month Changi had been surrounded by barbed wire and the Japanese announced that anyone trying to escape – and all suspected of helping the escapee – would be executed. There was much talk of the chances of getting away but such were the dangers that General Percival felt it necessary to issue an instruction pointing out that, while it was the duty of every officer and man to attempt to escape, an escape should only be attempted when proper plans had been made and the chances of getting away were good. I know of no escapes which were successful after the surrender of Singapore. The chances of a white man escaping detection were very small and, while the Chinese in general were sympathetic to us and suffered horribly at the hands of the Japanese, there were other local inhabitants only too ready to give one away.

At the beginning of March we were ordered to remove all badges of rank except for one star on the pocket. We also got very comprehensive instructions about saluting all Japanese personnel, saluting in the normal way if one was wearing a hat, otherwise halting and bowing low from the waist. It was unpleasant but one just had to take it. Failure to salute a Japanese guard in a manner which he considered to be appropriate usually resulted in a beating; to this day I react very violently to being slapped across the face – even by members of my family in a spirit of fun. If the Jap guard found it difficult to reach his victim's jaw he made him kneel and could then do the job properly with his rifle butt. The Japanese had a dreadful inferiority complex and the taller the British officer happened to be the more likely he was to get a real thrashing. I suppose I was lucky being of medium height but a good friend of mine, Major Grazebrook, who stood about six feet three inches, was picked on at every possible opportunity. It was so galling to have to stand aside and see one's friends and colleagues subjected to all sorts of inhuman treatment – anyone who tried to intervene was dealt with very severely.

During May we had an example of the sort of treatment everyone, no matter how senior, could expect. My diary recorded that, on 11th May, just as we were about to start our evening meal, a posse of Japanese arrived and bundled General Percival into a car. He wasn't allowed to take any spare clothes. He had previously been asked to supply technical experts to repair anti-aircraft guns; naturally he refused to do so, saying that this was not a fair demand. We did not see the General for fifteen days and naturally became very worried about him. All enquiries were met with blank stares from the Japanese. When he returned he told us what had happened.

In the camp office a Japanese officer repeated the request that the technicians should be provided and, when General Percival refused, he threw his papers onto the floor and leaped about the room shouting and screaming, 'Do you refuse to obey the orders of the Imperial Nipponese Army?' The General said that he fully expected to see the officer draw his sword and finish the matter there and then but soon he was in a car and taken to a cell in Changi Jail, where all the civilian internees were held. He was in a small cell in solitary confinement and for three days saw no-one, nor did he get any food. After some days he said he wanted to see the officer and a typical compromise was reached; the Japanese officer was happy that we showed him the sites of the anti-aircraft guns at the time of the surrender. A gun of that calibre is not the easiest thing to conceal. Even though the deal was celebrated over a glass of whisky the Japs could not miss the opportunity of keeping the General in solitary confinement for another two weeks – but he did have proper food and reasonable comforts. He was remarkably cheerful when he returned to our mess and told me all about this painful experience during one of the long walks we took around our prison perimeter.

At about this time I had my first bout of illness, a very sore throat and a fever together with a terrible feeling of debility. I spent long periods in bed and was feeling very sorry for myself; after some time it was diagnosed as dengue fever – and the only cure was to let it run itself out of the system.

Every effort was made in Changi to keep in touch with the other senior commanders and we went to great lengths to provide them with a good meal when they came to eat with us in the evening. It got more and more difficult to provide them with a glass of whisky or gin but it was incredible how much seemed to appear when we were really down to the last drop. They, on their part, gave us some really enjoyable meals on the meagre rations to which we were reduced. We still had our car and managed to scrounge the odd gallon of petrol.

After the war, I went for a walk over the fells in the Lake District; our home was near Penrith, and I saw the Shap Wells Hotel where German and Italian generals were imprisoned. I could not help but draw the comparison between the comparative luxury of their accommodation and the squalid quarters allotted to our senior officers. During July we had another example of the avowed policy of the Japanese to make it as difficult and uncomfortable as they could. Even though some working parties had been sent to Thailand and Japan, thus relieving the pressure on quarters, we were ordered into a smaller house and four more officers were added to the strength. It made life very difficult and tempers easily became strained. Added to all our troubles, the few batmen we were allowed started to go down with various tropical diseases. Medicines were short and it took a long time for people to recover. We began to see instances of beri-beri and other deficiency diseases, the only cure being good food and vitamin supplements. Malaria was also on the increase and we had very little preventative or curing drugs.

I managed to play a lot of bridge and it was a great solace to me during my captivity. I learnt to play the game at Oxford and in Changi we had a lot of fun playing matches against the other commands. While we spent a lot of effort entertaining ourselves, our main concentration was the pursuit of food and drink. We were able to spend our diminishing dollars in a canteen set up by the Japanese and were delighted when we were able to purchase fresh food such as eggs brought in from Singapore. Now and again we got some fresh meat in our rations but gradually rice became our staple food – with very little else.

I managed to track down many of my friends who had been captured and it was a great day when I saw my British Adviser, Mr. de Moubray, who had been wounded and captured with the Australian Division. He was still in hospital when General Percival visited them; he had a long talk with de M., who said he had some news from Mrs. de M. who had been interned in Changi Jail where she was not too well. Many military prisoners of war, particularly those who were members of the local volunteer forces, had wives and other relatives in the civilian internment camp. The Bishop of Singapore, The Right Rev. Leonard Wilson, who was allowed a measure of freedom by the Japanese, did marvellous work bringing messages from one side to the other. His exploits brought him under suspicion and he was subjected to brutal treatment and solitary confinement. How, you may well ask, could a civilised nation do this to a Bishop of our church?

The Japanese were extremely secretive about what was to happen to us. I think that very few people knew about future plans but it did give rise to widespread rumours – a feature of our life as prisoners of war, some were optimistic, some very pessimistic. Throughout the next three years we had the greatest difficulty getting true news – and when we did get it we had to be very careful with it so that our sources would be protected.

Just before my twenty-second birthday on 25th July, we heard that we were about to be moved away from Singapore – probably to Japan. I noted in my diary that cigarettes were short and I only had ten to last a week – as a reformed smoker I look back on those days with nostalgia!

Chapter 7

Move to Formosa

Having issued orders that we were about to move to Japan, the Japanese distributed rations such as we had not seen since we were captured. Unfortunately, when the move was postponed they did not send any more food to our camp, and we would have gone hungry had I not put a certain amount in a sort of crisis store.

About this time we had our first 'medical inspection' and this revolting procedure was repeated every time we moved from one place to another. I will burden my readers only once but I think it is right that you should appreciate the indignities we were forced to suffer. We were all lined up and made to bend over in front of a Japanese medical orderly – equipped with mask and horn-rimmed spectacles. A glass rod was then pushed into one's anus, extracted and shaken around in a test tube. What good this did I do not know because, after all the 'medical examinations', and I went through a great number, I never saw any action taken. There was much muttering of, 'Ah, so, ah so', and hissing through the teeth, but nothing ever happened.

We had been alerted for a move on the 17th July and it took place on the 16th August; this was a further example of the efficiency of the Japanese, for they never seemed to know what was happening to us. On the other hand, they were so secretive that, had they known, they probably would not have told us. During that month of waiting we had the usual shambles about the rations, too many one day and too few the next.

There was much time to speculate on the transport which was to take us away from Singapore, to a destination as yet unknown. Some thought it would be a converted Japanese cruise ship, others had heard that the Japanese Navy was accepting responsibility and we would travel in one of their vessels. These thoughts were well wide of the reality.

47

On the morning of our move we all went to celebrate Holy Communion and were then loaded into lorries for the trip to Singapore Docks. I think the Japs thought that there would be some hostile reaction from the local population as we were driven through the streets but there was none – quite the opposite, there was much sympathy for our plight but the Chinese dare not express it for fear of reprisals. When we arrived at the docks we saw the awful truth, a converted cargo ship with 500 crammed into a hold that could hardly accommodate a tenth of that number. The hold had been converted by putting in platforms one above the other. Nine of us had a space which measured six feet by ten feet, with a headroom of about two feet. It is difficult to visualise how cramped this was but just try to mark the measures out in your sitting room. The next day we were moved to another ship with the same sort of accommodation. I noted in my diary that I felt terribly sorry for the General; I also felt bloody sorry for myself. We lay at anchor in Singapore harbour in the most dreadful conditions, the hold was closed at night, there were no washing facilities and the sanitary arrangements were two planks projected over the stern of the ship. Never in my most awful dreams had I thought that I would be subjected to such inhuman treatment.

When we had to change ships so soon after being loaded on the first one, I could not make up my mind whether it was inefficiency on the part of the Japanese or just another example of their bloody-mindedness and desire to inflict the maximum pain and discomfort on all of us. We had been forced to put all our precious belongings into the size of pack we could carry and the heartsearching was dreadful as I had to decide what to take and what to leave behind. I remember carrying the General's pack and one belonging to a most likeable Brigadier Richards; I was very grateful to Sergeant Crockett, the General's batman who saw that my kit was put on board. Crockett was the finest type of British soldier, always smart in the most difficult circumstances, willing to help anyone and never complaining about the dreadful conditions. I know General Percival thought a lot of him.

We lay at anchor in Singapore for two days and it really was unpleasant. A lot of people had developed dysentery, which is a most distressing disease and one which is transmitted rapidly in a confined space. One loses almost all control over one's bowel movements and, as we were allowed only half an hour on deck every two hours, many people were in a critical condition. The Japanese knew this and did nothing about it. General Percival had developed symptoms of this complaint and the Japs did move him to share a cabin with one of the officers. We did not have much contact with the Japanese Navy Officers but they always seemed to be a class or two above the Army brutes we met.

The food on the ship was awful, twice a day we got a handful of rice and a few vegetable slops. We were promised bread but none ever arrived, perhaps for the best as we sweated so much in the cramped conditions that every mouthful of water was welcome. We set sail on 20th August and soon ran into a rainstorm, which cooled the ship but made it very cold for our brief walks on deck, and those of us who had suffered from malaria soon went down again.

On the 22nd we arrived off Saigon and hoped that we might get some better food but we did not. It was quite awful but one had to force it down in order to provide the fluid which was so essential in the heat of our hold. We sailed a day later and soon the ship began to pitch in the choppy seas and that made our lives even more uncomfortable. There were no lights in our hold and to get to the latrine was almost impossible – how we longed for an end to that voyage.

The end came on the 29th when we arrived in a port on Formosa in the morning. It seemed very clear that we were not expected and the rumour went round that it would be at least three days before we disembarked. We did, however, get a reasonable meal that midday and we were allowed a little more freedom to walk about on deck and see the port.

On the next day our miserable baggage was off-loaded onto the quay and we were told that we would be moving soon. When we did move we had to carry our kit on a three-mile walk round the town with ten minutes rest in every hour. This was another example of Japanese brutality as lorries which subsequently took us to a train could quite easily have picked us up at the docks. But, as we were marched round the town of Takao, the civilian population was forced to line the streets and witness our humiliation. But, it was evident that the sympathy of the locals was with us and not with the Japanese. This sympathy did not, however, extend to the Formosan guards who formed the majority of the staff in the camp at Heito, which was our destination. It was a feature of our captivity that we were usually guarded not by Japanese but by local troops, with the Japanese forming the administrative cadre of the camp. The locals obviously thought that much credit would come to them the more they hounded and beat up the P.O.W.s.

When we arrived in Heito we were lined up on the parade ground in front of the huts which were to be our homes for a long time. There then followed an incident which we came to appreciate had been followed in every camp in Formosa, Siam and Japan. The Japanese Army Headquarters in Tokyo had decided that every prisoner of war would have to sign a declaration that he would obey all the rules and regulations of the camp and that he would not try to escape. General Percival was asked to step forward and sign the declaration; this he refused to do and was promptly hauled off to the guard-house and put into a cell. All the rest of us were kept standing on the parade ground; many men were weak after the journey and soon collapsed. After prodding with a bayonet the guards seemed to accept that they were not putting on an act and allowed them to remain stretched out on the ground.

After three hours of standing it began to get dark and it started to rain; it was a miserable situation as it was clear that the Japanese were going to keep us there until we signed. In the end, General Percival was allowed out of the guard-room to talk to his senior military and civilian colleagues and it was decided that we should all sign the declaration as, given under such circumstances of duress, it could not be binding on the individual.

But, what were the chances of escape? The Japanese, wherever I was held, were obsessed with the idea that our only aim was to break out of the camp and run away. It would not have been difficult for anyone to jump over the flimsy perimeter wire of our camp but what chance would a white man have had in the countryside? We spoke not one word of the local language and very soon would have been given away by the local population. As my command of the Japanese language improved I was at pains to try to determine why the Japanese put such concentration on this escape business. I never got a satisfactory answer except that it was orders from Tokyo.

Our camp in Heito was a former labour camp for labourers employed in a neighbouring quarry. It consisted of a number of huts built out of bamboo and attap – a roofing material formed out of coconut palm fronds – not particularly waterproof. We slept on a straw mattress on wooden benches. Fortunately the climate in Formosa is temperate with no extremes of hot and cold and the humidity is bearable. Our only real problems came when there was heavy rain which flooded the camp, overflowed the latrines and soaked all our belongings. We had some spectacular thunderstorms which resulted in the camp being inches under water.

For the first few days in Heito Camp very little happened. We got minimum rations of rice and vegetables and our own private stores of tins were rapidly running out. The news soon came that the Generals were to move to another camp and they made every effort to take their personal staffs with them, but the Japanese were adamant and we stayed put. My diary recorded, 'Sunday 6th September. Here we are and here we stay. Oh, God. Padré allowed to celebrate communion and evensong. Brig. Goodman bellyaching about the quality of the food.' Most of our senior officers set a marvellous example to the rest of the prisoners but some could not come to terms with their changed situation.

When we arrived in Heito the Governor of Singapore, Sir Shenton Thomas, was very ill with dysentery and he was taken from the camp into a civilian hospital in the town, and promised special treatment. He returned a week later not much better; he had had no treatment and had been forced to work as a medical orderly. At this time we were inoculated against dysentery every three days but it did not seem to make much difference. Soon I was identified as a dysentery carrier and moved to a special isolation hut – the one advantage being that few Japanese or Formosan guards came anywhere near us.

The seriousness of our position soon began to be reflected in the number of people dying; my diary recorded –

'September 8th, Lt. Col. Kennedy and Capt. Walker died today.
September 10th, Lt. Kemlo, R.E., died early today.
September 13th. Rumour that Mr. Howell, the Attorney General of Singapore, had died in Heito civil hospital. Confirmed the next day when the padre was asked to collect his ashes. H.E. very upset.
September 18th. Griffiths, R.E., died today.

At about this time we were told that all orders would be issued in 'Nippon-Go', the Japanese language, and we would be expected to reply in it and understand. I quickly came to the conclusion that the sooner I learnt a smatter of the lingo, the better it would be for me. But, again one came up against the deep-rooted suspicions of our jailors; why did I want to learn more than was really necessary?

From that date, every night we were subjected to the most ludicrous but disrupting procedure. We had to appoint a hut monitor, who was responsible for recording where everyone was at a particular time. The report in Japanese went, 'Forty men in the hut, two men at the latrines, five men in the sick hut – total: forty-seven men.' If the figures did not add up all hell was let loose and the whole camp likely to be turned out so that a complete roll-call could be taken. The Formosan goons were not particularly numerate, we had great difficulty with the language in the early stages and it could take an hour or so in the cold night to satisfy the Japs that no-one had done a bunk. In Heito we had an absolute pig of a camp commandant called Lt. Tomaki and he was quite likely to come back to the camp in the early hours of the morning and turn everyone out of bed to count the troops.

In September, we were faced with the instruction that all officers and other ranks would be treated equally and all would have to work. We pointed out that this was in conflict with the provisions of the Geneva Convention but our commandant said that it was orders from the High Command in Tokyo – and in any case he knew nothing about Geneva or its convention. We tried to reach a compromise because there was a lot to do that could help our men, like carrying food and water for them, but we were ordered to get to the shovels like everyone else. The work was hard and it was awful to see how the Japanese insisted that a certain number of men would be at work every day, no matter how many men were on the sick list. One had to be at death's door to escape the morning muster. Some days we worked from six in the morning until six at night with only water, a handful of rice and a spoonful of sloppy vegetables to sustain us. The work was loading trucks with stones which had been quarried and moved to the side of the railway track. We filled bamboo baskets with the stones, carried the baskets forty or fifty yards and threw the stones into the trucks. The guards set a quota of trucks to be filled and we stayed until that quota was reached. I think that period was easily the worst in the whole of my captivity. It was particularly distressing to see sick men having to make up the numbers demanded by the Japanese. This seems to have been a feature of all Japanese prison camps and it was very evident on the Siam railway, where so many died and the labour squads often were made up of men days away from death.

There was much excitement at the end of September when we were told that a Japanese Lieutenant General was to inspect our camp. Soon after this news we were given a ticket with our names in Japanese and English to hang round our necks on a string. We also got the information that our heads were to be shaved in the interest of hygiene. I think that by this time we were past caring and hoped that the Good Lord would give us the strength to survive all the brutality and indignities heaped upon us. In the event, two days later we got the glad tidings that we were to be spared head shaving.

The Governor of Singapore had been in our camp since his release from hospital in Heito town but he was warned to be ready to move to join General Percival and the other Governors. My diary records that he gave me a very precious jar of Horlicks before he left and that he took a note for me to General Percival. Japanese efficiency prevailed; the Governor left in the morning, was back in the afternoon but left for good the next day. It was sad to say goodbye.

I always thought that the British Army could get a little up-tight when a General was about to carry out an inspection but it was nothing to compare with the near panic which struck the Japs. On the Sunday we were on parade at 5.00 a.m. We had about five practice musters throughout the day and finally a Colonel came to cast his eye over us. He was satisfied with the performances, to the extent that all the men – but not the officers – got four cigarettes. To their great credit the men had a whip-round and saw that their officers who smoked did not go without. I had nothing but great admiration for the British troops and the way they behaved during captivity.

On the Monday we had an inspection by a Japanese Lieutenant-General and it was quite a show. There was an incredible amount of shouting, swords flashed and there was much strutting and posturing by the camp guards. It was like a scene from a poorly produced *Mikado*. We acquitted ourselves so well that the men got three bananas each – the officers nothing. But, once again, we were not forgotten by our troops.

Our lives became monotonous and difficult and my diary records our concentration on food and the problems of getting enough to stay alive. Many times we attempted to set up deals with our Formosan guards, bartering items of clothing or a precious watch for foodstuffs. But, it was a hazardous undertaking: to be found out meant severe punishment for them and for us.

During December we had a new Japanese officer who visited the camp and seemed to assume a certain amount of authority over the dreaded Tomaki. Lt. Heoki was a small man, even by Japanese standards, and always seemed to be in danger of tripping over his sword. When he first came to visit us he sought me out and said that General Percival was well and hoped that I was fit. His English was passable and we soon learned not to make disparaging remarks in his presence. He did seem to have some influence on the way we were treated and he actually ordered that a Formosan guard should be beaten for ill-treating some of our sick men. We could hardly believe our eyes when we saw this happening.

By the end of 1942 the officers were working most days, either loading trucks with stones or on a pumping fatigue which provided the water for our camp. Boreholes had been sunk and equipped with not very efficient pumps but it was not a particularly arduous task. Much depended on the attitude of the guard assigned to look after us. On 4th December I wrote,

'Day on the pump. Very interesting time with guard. Got twenty cigarettes and some fish powder from him. Got some quinine at night. Good
news in the papers confirming what we heard elsewhere.'

One did not form many close friendships in camp, probably because one
was so concerned with personal survival, but I did meet and become very
friendly with John Meade-Waldo-Van, a Captain in the Leicestershire
Regiment. His surname caused many problems with the Japanese as they
attempted to get a list of prisoners in our camp. John was a gentle, quiet
man who bitterly resented the treatment dished out to us by the Japanese;
he was particularly upset by the brutal acts of the guards and his inability
to do anything about it. He was not a very practical person but I was able
to help now and again. My mother taught me to cook and she also insisted
that my brother and I learnt the rudiments of sewing and darning. Many
working shorts I was able to make for my friends out of rice and flour
sacks which we begged from the Japanese storekeeper. Anything was
better than wearing our own precious uniforms.

Working outside the camp gave us the opportunity to make limited
contact with some of the locals. The work we were doing was to provide
stone for some contracting project and now and again the civil engineers
responsible for the project would visit the site. On Monday 21st December my diary had the good news, 'Working on the trucks again but I
managed to get an egg. Had it fried, was it marvellous.'

Our first Christmas approached and everyone wondered how many
more we would have to suffer. Christmas Eve was marked by one of our
squads being accused of 'bad discipline', so Lt. Heoki and the Sergeant
Major administered a beating to everyone – not a particularly good start to
the festive season. On Christmas day we dressed up in our best uniforms,
the padre looking very smart in his vestments to celebrate communion and
we had reasonable food. The menu was:

6.15	Sweet tea
7.00	Misu soup, rice, orange, sweet tea.
11.00	Sweet tea, three slices of bread, half a pot of tomato jam, three biscuits.
4.00	Goose soup, slice of goose, potatoes, cabbage and beans. Fried bread. Fruit pudding with sake sauce. Orange.
6.00	Sweet tea, two buns, two bananas.

As you can imagine, this feast was as good as dinner at the Ritz in
comparison with our usual rice and vegetable slops.

Early in 1943 we were visited by the civil police and everyone was finger-printed and photographed. No-one told us why this was done but it appeared that it was part of the great escape game. At the same time we were introduced to one 'Sergeant George Myazako member of the Kempeitai – the Army Secret Police'. George was an American-Japanese from San Francisco who was on holiday in Japan at the outbreak of war and immediately pressed into service. His English was perfect but we never knew where his sympathies lay and we had to be extremely careful in our dealings with him. He did seem to be concerned about some of the more extreme brutal acts of the guards and now and again we managed by inference to suggest that he could do something. Soon we saw examples of the extraordinary authority and power of the Kempeitai; it was nothing to see George slap the face of a Captain in the Japanese Army and I saw him verbally abuse a Colonel who took it like a dog admonished by his master. It was, to say the least, an unusual state of affairs.

On the other side of the coin, we had to be guarded in our responses when George breezed into the camp and asked, 'So what do you think of the news from Russia?' 'What news?' Clearly George suspected that we had a source of news but it was absolutely vital that we gave no clue that it existed. Our two main sources of news were a clandestine radio and Japanese newspapers. I was never sure who ran the radio; it had been constructed by experts while we were incarcerated in Changi and components could be obtained with a minimum of trouble. I did know that the main part of the set was in the false bottom of a British Army water bottle, the head-phone was separate and the batteries yet another part. It was always kept in pieces and only operated on a very limited basis; for some time it was hidden in the walls of our huts and never in our personal kit which was subjected to random searches. The main problem came when it was necessary to arrange for the bits to be transported from one camp to another. The Japanese would never handle their own baggage and insisted that it was carried by the P.O.W.s, so the officer in charge of the radio detailed the Jap's kit where various pieces were to be concealed. It was not difficult to get the pieces in at the beginning of the journey but one had to move quickly to extract them at the other end. We did get firm news but it was distributed to a very limited number of our colleagues; during the war there was a propaganda phrase in England: 'Careless talk costs lives'; it was more than true in camp. Our other source of news was the Japanese press; very seldom did we get a paper in English and that was not very informative but we managed to purloin Japanese papers from their quarters. All menial tasks were given to the prisoners, such as cleaning the officer's quarters and sweeping out the kitchens. Everyone detailed to these fatigues was asked to pick up any Japanese papers, the more recent the better, without generating undue suspicion.

Having got the paper, it was another matter to translate what was in it. Like Chinese, the Japanese language is extremely difficult to read. There are no letters to form words and each picture character means something different. The language is not logical and unless you are a Japanese scholar you just do not know where to start. In our camp we had one officer who had a rudimentary knowledge of the script and, above all else, a very jealously guarded Japanese dictionary. In this way we managed to keep track of the main developments in the war, but for some months the news was not particularly encouraging.

February 1943 was perhaps the lowest point in my captivity. I had developed sores on my elbows and hands which did not respond to any treatment – not that we had much in the way of medicines – and I then began to show symptoms of beri-beri. This is a vitamin B deficiency disease, one's legs swell up, walking is difficult and passing water almost impossible. Ultimately the fluid rises into the lungs with the inevitable conclusion. I had managed to get a bottle of vitamin B tablets called 'Wakamoto' and I had kept them aside for such an eventuality but they did not seem to have much effect. I got steadily worse, my skin got tighter and tighter and I waited for the moment when I would be able to pass water properly. A sympathetic guard gave me some tomatoes and I wrote in my diary, 'Great pee started at night, went fifteen times and feeling much better. Legs improved.' Much has been written lately about the visions of those people who, for one reason or another, have been adjudged to have been close to death and then recovered. When I was very ill with beri-beri I was moved to the 'sick hut' which was an adjunct to the small camp hospital. Treatment was minimal but one was spared the constant harassing of the Formosan guards and the pressure to join the working parties. A distinct disadvantage was that the beds were alive with lice. I was puffing and blowing and had great difficulty in moving about; I remember lapsing into a semi-conscious state for quite some time and saw in front of me a dark tunnel with a shining river beyond, green fields and sunlight. It was a vivid picture and many people in a similar situation have reported the same sort of vision. I can remember it to this day. Once I recovered from the swelling and the excess of fluid left my body, I recovered slowly and never suffered from beri-beri again, but it was a frightening experience.

During the early part of 1943 Tomaki, our camp commandant, seemed to take leave of his senses. Every Sunday, which was supposed to be a rest day, he stormed round the camp shouting and screaming insisting that all officers turned out to work. We wondered whether, and of course fervently hoped that, the Japanese had suffered some major reverse but, with hind-sight, that did not appear to be the case. It was some time later that the first American victories at sea were achieved. No sooner had we settled down to a quiet game of bridge than it was broken up by that red-faced madman, who came out of the Japanese quarters like a jet-propelled swordsman.

My thoughts recorded in my small diary were almost entirely concerned with food – or the lack of it – and the activities of our camp staff. Onto the scene had come a Corporal Chiba, much taller and better-built than the normal Formosan, who set out to establish a reputation by beating up anyone his own size – particularly the unfortunate Major Grazebrook. At the same time we had news of the arrival of Red Cross supplies; but that is another chapter.

Chapter 8

On the Home Front

My parents were, of course, very concerned about my safety. One of the problems was that my father was in Nigeria and my mother at home in Penrith, Cumberland. I managed to send a telegram to my father on 27th December 1941 saying that I had escaped from Trengganu and that I was going to Singapore. I promised to send more telegrams but, in the chaos of the fall of Singapore, nothing more got through. Like many other parents, mine tried all sources for news of me; they had seen the kindness which Sir George and Lady Sanson had given me when I arrived like a refugee in Singapore. My father managed to trace them through the Foreign Office and Lady Sanson sent him a letter which is dated in November 1942; in Trengganu I had been known as 'Pat', as my British Adviser was also 'George'. I reproduce the letter in full. Lady Sanson was American, which accounts for some of her references.

Maryland.
U.S.A.
18th November 1942

Dear Mr Patterson,

Your letter of 20th October has just reached us, and I hasten to reply. We have so often thought of your boy, as we got so fond of him. I saw him last on 29th or 30th January and got away myself the following day to join my husband who was by then in Java on General Wavell's staff. From there we got down to Melbourne via Perth, and subsequently to San Francisco. So we were among the lucky ones. Pat was doing most awfully well, and in a charming boyish way informed me that he was one of the youngest Captains in the Command – at all events he was a Captain on the staff, and of great use at H.Q. because of his previous training in gunnery and his Malay language on top of it. He had done remarkably well in the language, and certainly is a boy who knows how to make himself useful in any way which shows itself. We are both AB-SOLUTELY CONFIDENT that he will be all right during this time of captivity. His gifts of getting on with people will stand him in good stead with the Japanese. And though I am not for one moment saying it isn't a hateful experience to have to undergo, we do truly feel his chances are good. We have heard very little news of the last three or four days before the fall, and very practically nothing since. One item which did percolate was exceedingly comforting. This was that the Japanese Commander held up the entry of his troops into Singapore town for several days after it fell. That was a blessing after the very severe fighting, which was what caused the bad doings in Hong Kong. We know the Japanese well, having spent many years in Japan; and we do both feel that one of the characteristics one must allow for is . . . how shall I put it . . . a strong desire to behave in a proconsular manner. It is not for nothing that one of the most read books during the last ten years or so amongst the enlightened military was Cromer's *Egypt*. There is no good in the beastly ones . . . vain, horrid and cruel. But the vanity (or pride) of most of them is not likely to permit them to behave badly after the first passion of conquest at all events. Nanking taught them a lot; taught them what we thought of them. I have little doubt myself that a fellow like Pat is managing to get used by them in some way – either in regard to the local peoples or the British soldiers. The only thing that is ever quoted about our poor fellows is that they make (or rather, I suppose, repair) the roads. Actually I should imagine the Tommies are better doing that than nothing at all, wouldn't you? Even allowing for inevitable exceptions. They are in fine condition, and though Singapore is hot and very damp, it really is a healthy place on the whole. The Japanese are mad on sanitation also so they are not likely to let down the previous high standard of anti-malaria. The whole tragedy was an agony to contemplate, and I confess that by the time I arrived in this so-untouched country, I was in a state of acute wretchedness. But one hears now, for instance, that chances are the food is not short, as it certainly was in Hong Kong . . . so one feels that the chances of our fine fellows are tolerably good at all events.

What the future will bring, when we get to pushing the Japanese back, that one cannot tell, but I don't really believe there is a need to be unduly pessimistic about even that. If we retake Burma, anything may happen. Certainly the Chinese, or at all events great numbers of them, will turn and rend the Japanese when the moment arrives. It was a tragic campaign. But on our intimate knowledge of the general Pacific set-up, three main things, we feel, emerge: (1) The fall of France has doomed the place for all the reasons we know. (2) Pearl Harbour puts the seal on, as the help which did in fact save Australia could not be in time to help Malaya or the Indies. (3) Here were mistakes . . . doubtless a-plenty, but not all to the degree the American journalists made out: in fact, consciously or no, they put up a smoke-screen for their own inadequacies. As many knowledgeable ones are now the first to admit. History only can say whether we should have saved Malaya (by planes which were pitifully few), by not fulfilling our promise to U.S.S.R. (which we did absolutely) or bombing German production plants less, or concentration less on Africa. It seems clear we could not do everything absolutely. I personally think that in these awful circumstances, Singapore had to take it.

We are now at the Embassy here, where my husband is Minister for Oriental Affairs (which means largely post-war). You will doubtless hear anything we hear about Singapore from the War Office or the Colonial Office but I shall keep your address, in case any small titbit got through in due course, and I would at once let Mrs. or Lady . . . so sorry I forgot) Patterson know. I partly come from your country, and adore it. I am sending this by air enclosed in a letter to my sister, who will send it on.

I don't know how much Pat was able to tell you of his dramatic escape from Trengganu in the early days of the war. By great luck I came upon him in the town at the end of it, dirtyish and very tired, but he assured me that in any case he would have telephoned me. He escorted about eight persons of both sexes through the jungle and down rivers, and I know not what, having wound up affairs in the Residency before leaving. His 'boss' was a highly nervous man, not at all the sort to deal with this kind of emergency, and there is no doubt that the stalwart Pat was able to do a great deal. He will tell it you all in due course. I can't think of any more details of special interest . . . one of the most appalling things that happened just before the fall was that the ships, which had to be got away of course, and were therefore laden with fleeing people, largely women, underwent fearful bombing, and hundreds . . . how many I doubt if anyone knows . . . were drowned. Four magnificent women with whom I was associated in odds and ends of work were lost – women with a Geneva background and all that implies. Simply heartrending. Better from your point of view that Pat had to stay. All the Civil Servants stayed . . . it was arranged in Council some time before the fall. My husband would be there if the General had not sent for him, as he was by then a member of the War Council, though actually we do not belong to that service . . . he was doing MEW work there. Oh dear, how sad it is. I shall want in due course to hear all about Pat, and I hope in happy days he will come and look us up in Suffolk, where we have a house.

This African campaign will make a great difference to you and I have no doubt . . . yours is Nigeria, isn't it?

With kind regards, and much sympathy for your anxiety over your boy,

Yours very truly,
KATHERINE SANSON

To J.R. Patterson. Esq.,
4 Carleton Terrace,
PENRITH,
Cumberland.

I had many invitations to visit people after the War but for one reason or another I found it difficult to take them up. My leave was taken up with seeing members of the family and catching up with their news and quite soon I found myself on a plane back to Malaya.

It is one of my greatest regrets that I did not manage to see General Percival again. He sent me a copy of his book *The War in Malaya* inscribed:

With my gratitude
and
Very Best Wishes
Arthur E. Percival
Lt. Gen.
G.O.C. Malaya 1941/42

Sept. 1949.

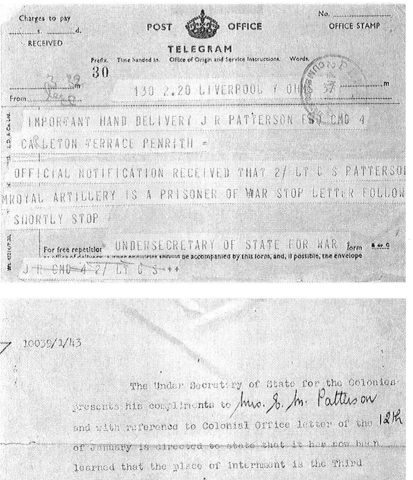

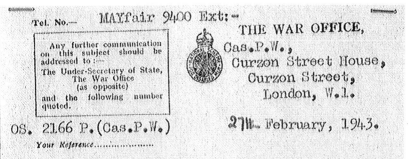

Tel. No.— MAYfair 9400 Ext: —

Any further communication on this subject should be addressed to :—
The Under-Secretary of State, The War Office (as opposite) and the following number quoted.

THE WAR OFFICE,
Cas.P.W.,
Curzon Street House,
Curzon Street,
London, W.1.

OS. 2166 P.(Cas.P.W.)

27th February, 1943.

Your Reference.......................

Madam,

    I am directed to thank you for your letter of 31st January and in reply to confirm that as stated in War Office letter of 28th November, 1942, Lieutenant G. S. PATTERSON, Royal Artillery is a prisoner of war in Japanese hands at the Third Branch Internment Camp at Taiwan.

    The letter from the Colonial Office (Enquiries and Casualties Department) stating that your son was at Malaya Camps was apparently sent to you in error.

    A further communication will be addressed to you regarding the question of your son's rank.

    The letter you kindly enclosed has been noted with interest and is returned herewith.

    I am,
        Madam,
            Your obedient Servant,

Mrs. J. R. Patterson,
   4, Carleton Terrace,
      Penrith,
         Cumberland.

Even though we had been captured in February, it was not until November that my family got firm news that I was a Prisoner of War. As I had been moved from Singapore to Taiwan in the August, it was not surprising that there was a certain amount of confusion about my location. Adding to the confusion was the fact that I was a Colonial Civil Servant who had gone back into the Army, so followed these communications.

Communications with home were sporadic and difficult. The first time we were allowed to write anything was on 20th June 1942 and, told to write not more than ten words, I wrote:

> Dear Mother,
>   I am well,
>   Love to all,
>   George.

> June 20 1942 179954 Captain G.S. Patterson.

Before we were able to write a short letter we were provided with pre-printed cards and, although they did not convey much information, they did have a recognisable signature on them.

In 1943 our treatment began to improve a little, beatings and face slappings were on a monthly rather than a daily basis. In August, exactly a year after we arrived in Taiwan, we were moved from Heito Camp to Shirakawa Camp. The accommodation was better and the regime very much more humane. The Japs were still hung up on this business of officers working and were very loath to give in on that principle. However, an acceptable compromise was reached; a number of us said that we were willing to work in the hospital looking after our own people; others agreed to provide working parties to tend the gardens inside the camp perimeter. The climate was excellent for growing vegetables but we had the unpleasant task of transferring the contents of the latrines, without further treatment, onto the plants. This was popular work as it gave access to the odd tomato when the crop ripened. There is no doubt that fresh produce saved a number of lives.

In September we were allowed to write a brief letter home, I was anxious to convey my concern about the health and whereabouts of my brother Hugh. He is four years younger and we had become very close because, with our parents in Africa, I was sort of responsible for him. We both went to a day school, The Royal Grammar School in Newcastle-on-Tyne, lodged with a family during the week and went to our Uncle and

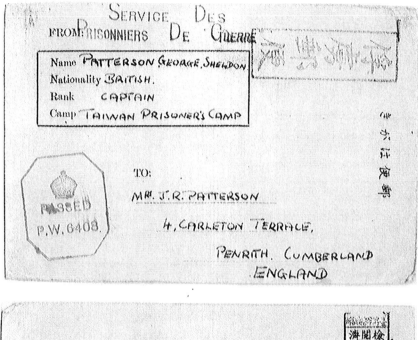

SERVICE DES
FROM PRISONNIERS DE GUERRE

Name PATTERSON GEORGE, SHELDON
Nationality BRITISH.
Rank CAPTAIN
Camp TAIWAN PRISONER'S CAMP

PASSED
P.W. 6408.

TO:
MR. J. R. PATTERSON

4, CARLETON TERRACE,

PENRITH. CUMBERLAND
. ENGLAND

IMPERIAL JAPANESE ARMY

I am interned in TAIWAN PRISONER'S CAMP

My health is excellent. usual. poor.

I am ill in hospital.

I am working for pay.

I am not working.

Please see that ALL THE FAMILY is taken care.

My love to you

George

Aunt at the weekends. Those years immediately prior to the war were very happy ones.

Our letters had to be written in capitals and, for the first few months, confined to one small page. They were brief and to the point.

September 1943

I am glad that I am able to write you a letter and hope that you have got the postcards I have sent. I am in good health and looking forward to seeing you all again sometime. I hope soon to have news from you. I wish I knew what my brother Hugh and father were doing now and hope that all the family are well. I have many friends here and we are very cheerful. We have had one lot of Red Cross stores and hope that more may come.

20th October 1943

I was delighted to get two letters two weeks ago. One from father of February 2nd and one from Peter Bentley. Please thank him. I am glad that Hugh was going to stay in Oxford and am looking forward to hearing the result of his examination. I wonder to which college he is going. Father seemed to have enjoyed his leave and I hope he has a successful tour. We shall have a lot to tell each other when we meet again. I am quite well and hope to get more news of you in my next letter.

That letter from my father, posted in Kano, Northern Nigeria, reached me in eight months but letters posted in England in November 1942 did not arrive until the end of March 1944 – seventeen months was about par for the course.

24th November 1943

The time has come for me to write you another letter and wish everybody a Merry Xmas and a particularly Happy New Year. I have not much to tell you this time but am hoping for another letter soon. I am quite well and cheerful. We are all looking forward to Xmas and my thoughts will be with you then. I hope Hugh has begun his university career and wish him every success. I am looking forward to dining with him in his college one day.

30th December 1943

My thoughts are now on the year which is just about to begin and I send you all my best wishes. I hope it will be a happy one for everybody. We had a good time here over Xmas and I expect you enjoyed yourselves at home. The weather would be different here, it is warm enough to go without a shirt during the day. Some parcels have arrived here and I hope I may get one from you soon with some letters. Being without news of one's family is one of the hardest things to bear in this life. My last news of Uncle Fred was that he had had an operation. I hope he has fully recovered and that he and Aunt Mac are well and happy. This is the first opportunity I have had to congratulate Miriam [my eldest cousin] on her 21st, I hope she has something she wants which I can give her on my return. Please give my best wishes and love to all at Hepscott [my second home] and to my Uncle Hugh.

One had to be very careful about what one wrote as the Japs just threw away any letter if they suspected that an attempt was being made to code a message. My 'Uncle Brian' was not a real Uncle but a very great friend of the family and a Commodore in the Royal Navy Reserve – one of the most senior officers in that force. My next letter expressed the hope that the Navy was doing its stuff. We knew that the Americans had made huge advances in the Pacific and we had more and more air-raid alerts, but we never saw a friendly plane.

3rd March 1944

I have no letters to answer. I wish I could hear news of Uncle Brian's new business, I feel sure it must be producing excellent results now. Give my best wishes to him and Aunt Doris. I look forward to seeing you all again. The weather here is perfect and my garden improves daily. I wonder if my brother is up at university or in the services? I hope he is well and happy. I am sure I will see a great change in him. Give my best wishes to Christo [a very old school friend] and all the boys. Love to the family.

My next letter home gave the family the good news that letters had started to get through in reasonable numbers but after a very long time. The letters to which I refer were posted in July 1942 – almost two years ago. But, it was still a marvellous day when they arrived. I don't think enough guidance was given by the authorities in England concerning the amount which should have been written. I got some wonderful letters from my parents, giving me copious news of all members of the family, but they took nearly two years to reach me. They had obviously taxed to the full the linguistic abilities of the censors and I would much rather have had a postcard with a few words. Indeed, at the beginning of 1944 many letters were returned as being too long and the authorities introduced a special Prisoner of War air mail post card. Even though I had moved camp three times since the card was written, one posted in September 1944 got to me in March 1945.

My mother was a wonderful person who brought up my brother and myself almost single-handedly as father was in Nigeria, a country with a reputation as being unsuitable for white children. I was twelve before she joined father for a limited tour and I never set foot in the country but my brother followed in father's footsteps after he had retired. Mother's organisation was always superb; she was one of a limited number of women who, in 1918, had been to a university and got a degree. In the very first letter she posted, she indicated that her letters would be numbered in series so I could soon see if any were missing.

30th March 1944

> Great joy. I had four letters yesterday, first two in Mum's new series, one from Hepscott and one from Dad posted in March. Fine news of Hugh and Dad's move. King's is a lovely college, I hope I will be able to visit him one day. All the family at Hepscott seem to be flourishing. I am very happy to hear about all of them. I am well and cheerful. My love to all and thanks for the good wishes.

I had a problem in that I did not know where my parents were. I knew my father was likely to be at his post in Nigeria and thought that my mother was likely to join him if at all possible. My next letter was sent to my aunt at my second home in Hepscott.

17th May 1944

> My dear Aunt,
>   Since I last wrote I have had eight letters from you, mother and Aunt Doris (the wife of Commodore Grant); they are joyfully

received even though more than a year old. I hope everybody is well and that Hugh is well wherever he may be. I am well and very cheerful. The weather is very hot at the moment. We have received our second issue of Red Cross stores and they are very welcome. My love to my parents and to all of you. I hope to see you all soon.

I knew that my aunt would let all other members of the family know that she had had a letter. With the lapse of time between writing and delivery, both ways, it was not easy to keep up a coherent correspondence. I was confined, from the first card from Singapore, to a limited number of words. I was delighted to get voluminous letters from my family and friends but fewer words and quicker transmission would have eased the pain of captivity.

My letter written in July contained another coded message. Before the war, my Uncle Fred lived in Paris; he was one of the last people to escape before the Germans occupied the place. My thoughts about him were to give a clue that we knew something about the progress of the war in Europe.

10th July 1944

I have had more letters from the family and from Raymond [an old school friend]. All the news is very cheering and joyfully received. I know you will be glad to get my letters and tell my friends that I am well and looking forward to seeing them all again. Investing my pay is a good idea, it will all come in very useful later. A big celebration is due for Dad's appointment and all the anniversaries. I hope Uncle Fred is well and can go home soon.

Letters were getting through to us during the second half of 1944, we were in a reasonable camp and it was clear that the Japs – even facing the awful problems of translation – were doing their best to distribute the mail. In November 1943 instructions were obviously issued that letters should be short and written in capital letters, these letters were followed by the airmail letter cards.

My last letter in 1944 acknowledged the news I had received that my parents had moved into a new house and, naturally, I wondered just where it was.

5th August 1944

More letters from everybody and a card in April arrived for my
birthday [July 25th]. I wonder where the new house is and I am
looking forward to hearing about it. I'm glad you can see Hugh on
leave and hope that he is well. Dad seems very happy. Give my
kind wishes to Brookes [a college friend] and thank Butcher for
his letter [see a later chapter]. My love to the Sansons, I have a lot
to tell them. I am well. Love to the family.

That really was the last letter I was able to write until we were released.
The Americans were making great advances in the Pacific and there was a
real danger of Formosa being invaded and the prisoners recaptured. The
battle of Leyte Gulf in the Philippines took place on 24th and 25th
October and that really saw the end of Japanese naval and air supremacy
in the area.

   At exactly that time General Percival and other senior military and
civilian personnel were suddenly flown from Formosa to Japan; there
followed a sea voyage to Korea and a train journey to a remote camp in
Manchuria.

Chapter 9

News from Home

I must begin this chapter with an illustration of a card which I received from my Uncle who was working in Nigeria. Quite independently he found his way to the same part of the world as my father, in a totally different field – he was a motor engineer. His card had obviously come to the notice of a keen Japanese philatelist, who cut off the stamps but was kind enough to write in the missing text.

23/12/44

JANUARY 16TH
FROM W. W. SHELDON
C/O JOE ALLEN & CO.
JOS
NIGERIA
BRITISH WEST AFRIC

DEAR GEORGE,

MY LENGTHY LETTERS

RETURNED NEWS EVERYONE AT HOME GOOD

YOU WELL AND CHEERFUL ALWAYS THINK

YOU LOVE UNCLE

When people heard that there was an address to which they could write, I got many letters from family and friends. I will not bore my readers with extensive extracts but two letters from contemporaries of my father in the Colonial Service in Nigeria were examples of the thoughtfulness of many people. This one, posted in September 1942, did not reach me until December 1944 but it had been to Singapore on its way.

The Residency,
Mbabane,
Swaziland,
South Africa.

24th September 1942

Dear George,

On my way across Africa I have seen that letters – very short ones – may reach you through the Japanese Red Cross. So I hasten to send a message of good wishes and I long to hear that you are safe. When your father went on leave he had not received any news of you. I saw your uncle in Jos at the end of August; he told me your father had arrived home safely.

I have also written to Bishop Wilson of whom his people have heard nothing.

After 21½ years I have left Nigeria on three years secondment to Swaziland as Resident Commissioner. That small territory lies between Transvaal and Portuguese East Africa and when I reach there I will write again because I shall be close to Lourenço Marques through which these letters probably go.

I do hope you are fit and well and that you have been able to get news home.

Your father told me of your trek from Trengganu and that you were again a gunner in Singapore so I have addressed you accordingly.

My best wishes
Yours aye,

Eric K. Featherstone

Lieutenant G. Patterson
Singapore Artillery

One letter which gave me particular pleasure was written by a friend of my father's with whom he had served for over twenty years in Nigeria. It illustrates the care which people took in writing to me, avoiding contentious subjects but doing all they could to be interesting. It also shows, I believe, the satisfaction which that generation took in writing good English. I make no apology for quoting the letter in full.

Hastings
3rd July 1943

Dear Patterson,

I have written many letters with this superscription, but they have always been to your respected father whom I first met at Maiduguri, I think it must have been in 1921. My excuse for writing to you is that you and your brother always formed a large part of our conversation whenever we forgathered in the evenings. I believe also that in those early days you used to know me as 'Uncle George'. So when I heard that you had the misfortune to be a prisoner of war, I thought perhaps it might beguile the monotony if you were to hear from me.

It's not too easy to know what to write about, as the most interesting things would undoubtedly be tabooed by the censor, so *faute de mieux*, I suppose I had better keep to personal matters.

The last time your father and I were together for any length of time was when we exchanged Provinces – he took over from me in Kano and I from him in Maiduguri. That was about six years ago, so that the last detailed news I had of you is considerably out of date. During his last leave – about two months ago – we got in touch again and he told me you had been up at New College, but had gone down to join up; which is exactly what happened to me in the last war when I was up at Exeter.

A talk on the wireless the other evening by Julian Huxley would have interested you. He was one time Fellow of New College and he was talking of Spooner, chiefly of course about his 'isms. Most of the old chestnuts appeared although I missed his priceless effort on Oxford station when he kissed the porter and gave his aunt sixpence – she, poor lady, was seeing him off. According to Huxley the only authenticated Spoonerism he perpetrated was when he told the old lady who was sitting in his Stall in Chapel, 'Madam, I regret to say that you are occupewing my pie.' The ungodly, you will remember, impiously added, 'but if you wait a moment the verger will sew you into a sheet.' I remember seeing him in Chapel, a tiny frail old man, but to my regret he never did anything exciting.

I was invalided three years ago with blood pressure and have had to take things quietly – although this is not one of the quietest of places. So now I delve in the garden and my wife keeps rabbits for the table. As a hobby I have started collecting early editions of the Classics. The one that pleases me most is a black letter Vulgate printed in Lyons in 1500, which by a stroke of luck I heard of just before its owner was consigning it to the salvage. I wonder what Schools you were reading? If Greats, then I might descant upon my treasures – otherwise I fear I should only bore you.

I suppose this is about all the Censor will stand for so I had better close down. I hope to be sending you *Punch* and, if you will let me know, anything else you would like.

So here's the best of luck and may you soon return home.

Yours sincerely

P. G. Butcher

I don't know what the Japanese censor thought of the black letter Vulgate; he didn't think it was code because he allowed the letter to get through without mutilation. I never got the *Punch* magazine and could not reply as the letter took over a year to reach me.

It was not easy to appreciate how worried people were at the lack of firm news about prisoners and the relief when something did get through. My father was on leave at the end of 1942 when the official news arrived that I was a prisoner of war. I am sure that the Red Cross did all they could to speed the transmission of information but they faced almost insuperable obstacles – particularly the opposition of the Japs. Two characteristics stand out in my mind; the Japs were suspicious of everything and secretive to the point of not telling anyone about anything. Some flavour of the relief people felt can be judged from this extract from a letter written by my father; he was not the most emotional of people.

'There was more than joy in the land on Wednesday night when I received from the War Office a telegram to say that official notification had been received by them that you were safe. Mum's and my own thankfulness at this news is impossible to describe. We telegraphed your brother Hugh and your Uncle in Nigeria. Hepscott, your Aunt says, went almost *en fête* and Morpeth [the local Town] buzzed with the glad tidings. Mum has had a letter this morning from Christo who had had the news from your cousin Miriam. Now our prayer is that you will keep fit for the day when we shall be able to renew the fellowship of heart and hand. Soon, it may be, we may receive some news in your own writing. That will be another great day. I am so glad that this news of you has come before I left home. I shall do that shortly and my next letter to you, in due course, will be from another place.'

My father had his own adventures during the war as his journey to and from Nigeria usually took him by air through Lisbon – a hotbed of spies. The family were always greatly relieved when he arrived safely at the other end. In these days of international telephone calls, instant connection by satellite to all points of the globe, it is difficult to realise that a telegram could take three or four days to arrive. It was, of course, much quicker than the one or two years that our letters were taking.

The next letter from my father was, indeed, from another place and so mucked about by the censor that it was difficult to get any sense out of it. His address had been obliterated with black ink and replaced by the legend 'P.O. Box 5499 Cairo Egypt'. I never found out where this was. The first paragraph must have referred to his journey from England and the black ink was so thick that it penetrated to the other side of the paper.

My mother was an excellent correspondent and most of her letters with news about the family got through without the attention of the censor's black ink. However, when it came to telling me that she had progress reports from father on his journey back to Nigeria – all the place names were inked out. It must have taken the censor hours to go through the letters and it was no bad thing when the postcards with limited texts were introduced. My poor mother had all the anxiety about me and also the worry as father went by sea in 1943. In one letter she wrote,

'I had a very anxious time about Dad last week on his perilous journey but had a cable on Monday saying he had arrived at the first port. I have had too much anxiety about you this year to be able to stand much more.'

She continued to write at least once a month, hoping that she would hear from me one day, but her letters kept me very up to date with news of the family.

Her letter of 22nd June 1943 reported the arrival of my first postcard: 'I have a lot to be thankful for – last Tuesday I had the first word from you that I have had since December 1941. It was only a field postcard but at least it had your own dear signature – the usual funny scrawl. It has been a long time to wait, but patience has its reward. We hope soon to have a letter from you but, better still, to hear that you are receiving letters from home.'

The long newsy letters ceased in September 1943 when, instead of two sides of family news, all I received was:

'Fourth card arrived Stayed Hepscott for Miriam's 21st birthday. Spent two days in London with Hugh now in pre O.C.T.U. 50th birthday today. Love. Mum.'

That letter took only a year to reach me and thereafter there was a gradual improvement, the last letters I got in camp took about six months.

My father, who had been made Chief Commissioner of the Northern Provinces of Nigeria, sent a short note from his new home in Government Lodge. Kaduna.

'Letters recently returned as over long. Sorry consequent gap news. Hope you well. Am in good health. News from home good. Love in heaps. Dad.'

His last postcard gave me the excellent news that it was from 'Sir John Patterson, K.B.E.' Posted in July 1945, it got to me before I was released in a matter of weeks rather than years.

Chapter 10

Food, More Food

Many of our thoughts and efforts were concentrated on getting enough food to keep alive. The Japs were working us, particularly the other ranks, long hours with very meagre rations. The main food was rice and very little with it. We were convinced that the Red Cross must have been trying to get parcels to us; it was obvious that the Japanese organisation would never be able to cope with parcels from individuals.

Our lives were pretty miserable, we had all sorts of stupid but irritating instructions. We were issued with clogs and made to hand in boots and shoes; the boots were handed out in the morning for work and handed in when the gangs returned to camp in the evening. All this took time and was quite pointless; just another example of the Japs believing that there was some chance of someone escaping.

With no advance warning my diary recorded 18th March 1943: 'Great day. Arrival of five trucks of Red Cross parcels. Spent time after tea unloading it. Wonder how much the Japs will take.' It did not take long to find out; the next day they removed fifty-three parcels to their own quarters. Our own rations were short and it was particularly galling to know that food was within reach while men were still dying in the camp. Some with serious attacks of malaria would probably have died anyway but a lot, suffering from deficiency diseases like beri-beri, would certainly have been saved. The Japs played cat and mouse with the Red Cross stores; the dreadful Tomaki told us that we could not have any parcels as orders from Imperial Japanese Army Headquarters in Tokyo had not been received. What an excuse, can anyone imagine that such instructions had to come from Tokyo? Ten days later we were told that it would probably take a month for orders to release the stores to reach the camp. Exactly a month after the parcels arrived we had our first taste of bully beef, but what a performance. The parcels, packed with a variety of tins such as syrup, spam, bully beef, creamed rice were supposed to be issued one parcel per man. But, the Japs didn't like that idea and decided that each tin would be opened in the presence of a guard and the contents used to bolster our rations in the cookhouse. I don't know whether they expected to find machine guns or grenades in the tins but their action took a lot of pleasure out of the parcels. The British soldiers were very critical and had almost got to the point of saying, 'If that is the way they want to behave, they can keep the bloody parcels.'

At the time we got the first distribution of Red Cross supplies, we had an inspection by an old senior officer. As was usual on these occasions, there was a tremendous amount of flap. We were up rehearsing at 5.00 a.m. and the old chap expressed extreme displeasure about everything except the working parties. As was the case whenever we had an inspection, the officers had to wear their best uniforms and there was no question of them having to work. Little by little the parcels were broken down and the tins opened in the cookhouse; every second day or so we got something, even though it might be half a bar of chocolate.

Even after the arrival of the Red Cross stores, deaths in our camp, mainly from malaria, continued to occur at an alarming rate. The Japs were pretty reasonable about allowing us to attend funerals, indeed the only time they showed much respect was when a man was dead. I tried to go to the burial service of the men I knew and it became an almost daily occurrence. It was a sad little procession that wended its way with one guard to the burial ground outside the camp perimeter. In my diary I recorded the deaths of

10th June	Gnr. Gourney R.A.
11th	Cpl. Vaughan Suffolks
12th	Pte. Thorpe R.A.S.C.
16th	Pte. Rayson Sherwood Foresters
18th	Pte. Thornley Recce. Corps
19th	Sgt. Nabbs 1st Cambs.
21st	Gnr. Gates 118 Field Regt.
	Sgt. Moran

Our doctors said that the Japanese authorities were very worried about the deaths and the high numbers of men who were sick and unfit to work. It did not seem to have much effect as they still insisted that a certain number went out of the camp each day 'up the line' to load the railway trucks with stones. Most of the deaths came after repeated bouts of malaria, some resulting in cerebral malaria which is almost incurable.

I had been doing work in the hospital and helped to prepare an extraction of chinchona bark which is a cure for malaria. It was a very rudimentary operation but we did get a solution which was almost palatable. At that time I was having a fairly high fever every second day; the weather did not help as it rained most days and it was very cold at night. I managed to keep my fever under control by taking four or five doses of our revolting potion. It kept the malaria at bay but it played hell with my stomach.

Working in the hospital, I often wondered why some men died and others, who seemed to be very seriously ill, survived. Some put up a long and courageous fight, others just turned their faces to the wall. With the very limited medical supplies, the doctors had the difficult decision to give the drugs to those who had the best chance of pulling through. I don't think the doctors made many mistakes and I was full of admiration for their dedication and the way they stood up to the Japs.

We had often been promised a visit from the Red Cross representative and one day it seemed to be very close. A number of men were picked out and told exactly what they could say. The visit of Dr. Paravicini was, on all such occasions, carefully staged. No-one was allowed to talk to him on an individual basis, all answers had to be taken off the prepared sheet, but nothing escaped him. He explained how difficult it was to get the supplies from East Africa and how strained the lines of communication were once the goods arrived in Japan. Dr. Paravicini could not have missed the poor state of our camp; we had had some weeks of rain and the inside of our huts was cold and wet.

We lived on rumours good and bad and soon heard that there was a proposed move of the majority of officers to a special officers camp. Some were to stay in Heito to help with the administration and there was much heart-searching wondering whether one was on the going or the staying list.

July 1943 was a month of mixed fortunes. It started badly with more deaths. Pte. Ferguson of the Suffolk Regiment died on the 13th and I noted in my diary 'that makes six this month and 45 since we came to this camp.' What a dreadful record! Spr. Wadsworth of 41 Coy R.E. died on the 15th, when we got firm news that some officers were definitely moving to another camp. The entry in my diary for 18th July said, 'Am on the list for the move. Thank God but unfortunately John has to stay.' I don't know how the Japs made the selection but it was grim to have to leave friends behind in the pretty certain knowledge that we might be going to a better camp, while there was very little prospect of an improvement in their miserable conditions.

Our kit was all packed up and then unpacked for a rigorous search; what the Japs expected to find I just do not know but every item of clothing was unfolded and shaken. Every piece of paper was examined in minute detail and I had a problem getting my diary to the next stage of my captivity. The morning of our departure arrived and the dreaded Corporal Chiba decided to take it out on those victims whom he would not see again. The Japs had a stave about five feet in length which they used in their martial arts games and exercises; it was incidentally an ideal weapon for assaulting the prisoners. Chiba set out on a calculated campaign of brutality. People were beaten for no real cause but he was not beyond inventing an excuse for a beating – if indeed an excuse was necessary. To bow in salute with a dip of the head was 'arrogance', to bow almost to the ground was 'insolence' and both merited a whack with the stave. Poor Major Grazebrook, Chiba's favourite, was beaten because he happened to be in sight and he was taller than Chiba – but only just. I managed to escape this mayhem and very thankful I was.

At last we were in lorries and moved to Shirakawa Camp where my diary records, 'new camp marvellous. All the brigadiers and colonels here but not General Percival or the senior civilians. All seem very fit.' The camp was a great improvement on Heito, the accommodation was much better and our buildings kept out much of the bad weather. It was a large area with the gardens inside the perimeter wire so all the work was done inside the camp itself. In Heito we had been subjected to the hassle of working parties having to go outside the camp with all the problems of roll-calls and perpetual checks to ensure that no-one had taken off for the countryside. We worked in the garden, I worked for some time in the hospital and then in the cookhouse. It was an officers' camp so we all had various tasks but nothing like the hard physical grind at Heito. Apart from working about one day in three, we were able to play bridge and generally amuse ourselves. I started to learn shorthand and Dutch – which I found a very difficult language and I didn't make a lot of progress.

The only drawback in the place was the food. We were always on very short rations, 'Because,' said the Japs, 'as you are not working for the good of Nippon, you cannot have working men's rations.' In the cookhouse we tried to make the meagre food palatable but it was not easy. I remember how highly prized was the burnt rice which stuck to the bottom of every cooking pot; each squad took it in turn to have this delicacy.

Chapter 11

Waiting and Waiting

When one is sentenced to a period of imprisonment in a Court of Law one has a pretty good idea just how long one is likely to be behind bars. One knows the length of the sentence and the likelihood of it being reduced on the grounds of good behaviour. No such calculation can be made by a prisoner of war; we tried to keep our spirits up by suggesting to each other that each day that passed had to be one day closer to eventual release but, on occasions, we did become very dispirited. One entry in my diary just said, 'Two years is an awful long time.'

Our lives were ruled by the attitude of the Japanese Officer who happened to be Camp Commandant at the time. In December 1943 I was made assistant to the American Colonel Pilet, who represented all the prisoners in negotiations and discussions with the Japs. At about the same time we got a new Commandant, Lt. Wakiama, who came with a pretty awful reputation. This was soon confirmed when he had the whole camp on parade and set out the various grades of collective punishment which he intended to apply for a series of offences – real and imagined. Our discussions with him were pretty pointless as our main concern was our food, or rather the lack of it. For weeks we existed on a diet of rice and a vegetable soup with no meat or fish; even so, without the dreadful fever that had haunted me for months, and not having to do heavy physical work, I began to put on weight. Of course, it was from a pretty low starting point: my normal weight was about 10 st. 7 lb., in October 1943 I was 8 st. 2 lb. and this went up steadily until June 1944 when I was over 9 st. Why the Japs insisted on weighing us every month I just do not know but it was part of an established routine for prisoner of war camps and it did provide a bit of light relief for us.

I mentioned earlier one Japanese officer called Lt. Heoki; he was about the only one who crossed our paths who seemed to have any spark of human kindness in his make-up. All the others were either sadists or completely indifferent to the fate of the prisoners in their charge. Heoki was small for a Japanese, his uniform always seemed far too big for him and his huge sword likely to trip him up at any moment. We never found out what his real role was, sometimes he was in direct charge of our camp then he would disappear only to come back weeks or months later in the guise of an inspector. He spoke a few words of English and I remember him coming to look specially for me to tell me that he had seen General Percival, who was well and sent me his good wishes. He also let slip the fact that the generals and senior civilians were no longer in Formosa but had been moved to Japan in October 1944. He had an engaging toothy smile, and while he had little authority to make changes, one always felt that he was listening with some degree of sympathy. The officers certainly had a somewhat easier time when he was masterminding the work pro-gramme. Part of my work was to pump water for the camp into a tank which was far too small for our needs. Heoki arranged for a bigger tank and a new feeder pipe, which made life a lot easier.

Apart from keeping alive, our main preoccupations were to keep sane and to try to garner as much news as possible about the outside world and the progress of the war. On their part the Japanese did their utmost to see that we did not get any up-to-date news and always attempted to make us believe that it was only a matter of time before the glorious Japanese Army and Navy would be victorious. We did get some hard news from infrequent use of our clandestine radio but had to be very careful to limit the number of people who were privy to this information. For the radio to have been discovered would have meant executions on a pretty vast scale. In his camp General Percival had been issued with a wireless receiving set which, naturally, could receive only Japanese stations. Even so, he and Mr. C. R. Smith, the Governor of British North Borneo, listened to the news and the military pronouncements and found they could pick out a certain number of names. They listened religiously four times a day and then spent hours attempting to make some sense out of their voluminous jottings. With practice they became remarkably successful and, until they were sent to Japan and then Manchuria, managed to produce a news-sheet every second day or so.

Our other source of news was Japanese newspapers. Sometimes we were given a very old copy of one of the two papers printed in English throughout the war, the *Nippon Times* and *Mainichi*. But it was much bet-ter for us to get a recent copy of the Japanese paper so that our interpreters with their precious dictionaries could get to work on it. I remember one occasion when Heoki was walking round the camp with the latest papers stuffed in the back pocket of his trousers. This was a very tempting package and required very quick thinking on the part of those who were in contact with him. We were responsible for the cleaning and general maintenance of the camp staff car and, while he was crawling underneath the vehicle to inspect some serious fault, the papers were quietly extracted and spirited into our quarters.

Wherever we went we managed to organise a library. Each man would take one or two books when we moved camp and, on arrival at the new camp, these would be put in some central pool. The Japanese regarded this as a simple pleasure and never interfered with our organisation. I have a record of the 250 books, starting with *Gone with the Wind* and finishing with *Oliver Twist*, which I read during the three and a half years of captivity.

We also got up to all sorts of games to pass away the time and fight boredom. We had little spare energy for physical sports but I remember spending a lot of time trying to establish whether or not 'thought transference' was possible. I tried this with an amazing character, Major John Nicholson, amazing because he had suffered months of serious illness which would certainly have resulted in death had it not been for his resolute, fighting spirit. The low point in his medical history was in October 1943 when his weight had dropped to 6 st. 6 lb. He was not a very large person but it was incredible to see him put on three stones in weight by June 1944, once he was cured of dysentery and beri-beri. In our experiment he sat with a copy of the Bible about 100 yards away and I tried to transfer through the air waves the chapter and verse I wanted him to identify. We did not, as far as I remember, ever get as close as choosing the correct Book but we did have a lot of fun and passed some more time. By the end of 1944 the Americans had captured many of the islands in the Pacific and our Japanese guards were getting more and more jumpy. We had many air-raid practices and were made to dig some trenches in our camp but we did not see or hear any Allied planes.

For much of the time we were too tired to do anything more than collapse on our bunks and sleep. The Japanese seemed to take a particular delight in making the officers toil until they dropped. But there were some moments when we sat and chatted about the prospects of release or the good times we had had in the past. The merits of beer brewed in Scotland were compared with those brewed in Burton-on-Trent. It was an extraordinary thing that people would sit for hours talking about restaurants they had visited and the splendid meals they had eaten, when all they could look forward to was a few spoonfuls of rice, salt and a vegetable soup.

In Singapore the person in charge of the catering at General Percival's household was one Sergeant Browne of the Army Catering Corps. His family had owned and run a restaurant and he had worked as a sous chef at the Savoy. Before we were shipped to Formosa and the Japanese left us pretty much to ourselves, I used to sit for hours talking about food and writing down the recipes which Browne remembered. I still have the two note books divided into sections 'Meat', 'Vegetables', 'Soups and Rice' and a host of others. He was a great enthusiast and had a phenomenal memory; to this day I can picture him demonstrating with a large spoon and water just how one glazed a fish with sauce.

When I could bring myself to talk about my experiences it was the amusing and interesting things I remembered rather than the general horror of our days in captivity. One of the first incidents I related to my family concerned the sergeant-major's horse. I believe that was the starting point of my daughters saying that I should put these stories down on paper.

We had very little cause for mirth and merriment and on many occasions, in order to avoid a beating, it was necessary to conceal our true feelings from our hosts. Such was the case when we had a visit from a Japanese sergeant-major who, I suspect, was a member of the dreaded kempeitai. He came to our camp in Taiwan fairly frequently and kept his horse in the camp. As the horse was never exercised it was just raring to go when the sergeant-major got on its back with the result that he was deposited on his back-side in the middle of the parade ground – much to the delight of the assembled prisoners-of-war who had the greatest difficulty not laughing their heads off.

After a week or so I summoned up enough courage to suggest to the sergeant-major that if the horse was exercised during his absence, he might avoid the spectacle of being deposited arse over tip in front of the captives. He said that none of the guards could be spared to exercise the horse and, in any event, he would not give the job to them. I suggested that I could do it and, of course, the immediate reaction was 'But you might try to escape'. I pointed out to him the chance of a white man running away with a horse in the middle of Taiwan. With his smattering of English and my very rudimentary Japanese it was agreed to give the project a trial but I would have to be accompanied outside the camp by one of the Formosan guards.

So I collected the horse on a leading rein and set out with one of the smallest of our guards who appeared to have been issued with a rifle that was at least three sizes too big for him. The guard soon got tired so we agreed that I would take the horse round in a circle and pick our friend up on the way back to Camp. This routine worked well and I became bold enough to accept some of the bunches of bananas which the local farmers pressed on me. There was a slight problem getting the bananas past the guard at the main gate but I managed to convince them that the horse had developed a taste for bananas and the sergeant-major, for whom they had considerable respect, would not be pleased if I had to report that his horse had been deprived of his favourite food. It took no more than seconds for the horse and bananas to be rushed to the stable and for the bananas to be transferred through the back wall to one of my friends waiting there.

All good things come to an end and too soon the horse and sergeant-major were transferred.

Chapter 12

Voyage to Japan

In February 1945 came the most unpleasant, and in retrospect, the most dangerous part of our captivity. The Japanese, in the last few months of 1944, had started to move Prisoners of War from the Philippines back to Japan. It was winter time and many of the captives had no warm clothing and suffered terribly during the journey. The Japanese never marked their ships with the Red Cross emblem so the Americans had no idea that in many cases they were bombing their own people. In his excellent history of the war, *The Rising Sun*, John Toland has a graphic description of the horrors suffered by Americans who were in the holds of the *Enoura-Maru*. When the bombs fell more than half of the 500 prisoners in one hold were killed outright, the carnage was indescribable and the dying and wounded were left for three days with little food and water and no medical assistance. The survivors were transferred to another ship, the *Brazil-maru*, which sailed for Japan on 14th January; many who had survived dysentery and starvation froze to death as snow fell through the open hatches. Every morning the call went up, 'Roll out your dead', and as many as thirty bodies were collected. In their diaries prisoners described the bodies, who 'all looked alike, teeth exposed in a snarl between lips, ribs almost bursting, sunken eyes and pipestem legs and arms.' Food and, more importantly, water was severely rationed; four men had to share a mess tin of rice and each got only one spoonful of water a day. Prisoners risked a beating from the guards as they attempted to lick the water which had condensed on the walls of the ship's deck engines.

Our journey was made in a convoy of two cargo ships escorted by two destroyers. There was the usual loading of the prisoners into cramped conditions in the holds, but it did have one advantage in that all the bodies tended to generate warmth! Our Japanese guards had obviously heard stories of the bombing of other ships and were not at all happy about the prospects on the voyage. One of our guards had a brother on one of our escorting destroyers and told me, when we got to Japan, that his brother had not arrived and his ship had been sunk by bombs or a submarine. We sailed mainly at night and crept up the coast. I remember being allowed up on deck to see Shanghai which seemed to be working normally. It must have been a marvellous sight in peacetime.

After two awful weeks we arrived in Moji. The camp itself was in a coal-mining area and we were not at all impressed with the accommodation, but we were told that it was a staging camp and that we would soon move on – but how many times had we been told that the next camp would be a health resort? My only recollection of the Moji camp is that it was very depressing and the men we found there were resigned to working in the coal mines. One day we were paraded through the streets; this was not unusual, but to be taken to the public warm baths was a treat indeed. The local people, particularly the Japanese women, tried to express their concern at our condition.

By the time we arrived in Japan, our treatment was better than it had been for some time. I even noted in my diary, 'No-one had been beaten for quite a long time.' Whether all this was the result of orders from above or whether the middle ranking Japanese officers had some premonition of what was to come we never knew.

In this connection it is pertinent to see what was happening in the outside world. We had little hard news but it was obvious that things were not going well with the Japanese and the odd 'gem' dropped by a guard helped us to build up a reasonable picture. When the battle for the Philippines was at its height, Imperial Headquarters ordered the repatriation of all prisoners of war to the Japanese mainland. At about the same time, November 1944, articles in the *Nippon Times* praised the treatment of prisoners of war by the Japanese while criticising the conditions in which German P.O.W.s were kept by the British. Our old foe from Singapore, General Yamashita, was commanding the troops in the Philippines and saw the last effective opposition to the Americans crumble in January 1945. Only Iwo Jima and Okinawa remained as fortresses between the advancing Americans and the Japanese homeland. While we were being taken from Taiwan to Japan, the Americans had begun their battle for Iwo Jima. It lasted until the end of March and the Americans lost nearly 5,000 men; of the fanatical Japanese defending the island, only 3,000 out of 21,000 survived.

Life has always been very precious to me and, as a Christian, I could never come anywhere close to understanding the Japanese attitude that it was better to commit suicide rather than surrender. The Japanese officers all looked down on us and could not understand why we had not shot ourselves rather than disgrace our families and ancestors by surrendering. There are many stories of Japanese rushing towards American troops pretending to surrender but having a primed grenade in their hands or tied to their waists. This practice resulted in the Americans being very loath to take prisoners – with very good reason.

Rather than shoot themselves, the Japanese preferred to commit 'hari-kiri', a ritual slashing of the abdomen and a slow painful death. In many cases a colleague brought their suffering to an end by administering a sword cut to the neck or a bullet through the head. It is so difficult for westerners to understand why the Japanese were so convinced that they would achieve greater glory in such a death rather than living and working for the benefit of their country. In the same way the 'kamikaze' pilots who flew their planes, loaded with explosives, into the side of enemy ships were making the supreme sacrifice with no hope of survival. No wonder they struck terror into gun crews trying to shoot them down.

These then, were the dedicated troops who defended Okinawa during the last months of our captivity. When the battle for Okinawa was declared over at the beginning of July after three months of savage fighting, much of it hand-to-hand, the Americans had lost over 12,000 men, the Japanese more than 110,000 and 75,000 civilians perished caught in the cross-fire between the two armies. War, indeed, is a terrible, pointless exercise.

While these momentous events were taking place in the Pacific, the Japanese mainland was subjected to ever increasing raids by American bombers. Each captured island brought the planes closer to Tokyo and tremendous damage was done by the bombs and resulting fires. Many Japanese homes were flimsy in construction and large areas were laid waste when a wind blew the flames after an air raid.

During all this we were taken to the camp which was to be our final place of incarceration – Hoten Prisoner of War Camp near Mukden in Manchuria. We were paraded once more on the dock-side, subjected to the usual farcical pantomime of the anal glass rod and then taken by over-night ferry to the Korean port of Pusan. Travel had to be over-night as the American bombers had established a measure of mastery in the skies and many Japanese ships had been sunk.

At Pusan we were loaded into quite reasonable carriages for our two-day train journey to Mukden. Food on the journey was provided in little individual boxes and we were quite surprised and pleased at the change in our circumstances – but very wary in case the improvements did not last. For once we were not confined to an airless, windowless hold and were able to see something of the countryside. The month was April – we had stayed only five weeks or so in Japan – the winter was coming to an end and there were signs of Spring. The country through which we passed appeared to be very fertile and we saw farmers preparing the land for the first planting. It is, indeed, a very fertile country and the farmers manage to get two crops from the land between the spring thaw and next winter's freeze. It was fortunate that we did not move until the warmer weather was on the way; Japan had been very cold but it would have been worse in Manchuria. The Japanese had issued us with a small amount of so-called warm clothing but it did little to keep out the biting winds.

Our camp at Hoten was a special prisoner of war camp rather than a makeshift conversion of a labourers' quarters. There were three very large multi-storied buildings which housed about 1,750 prisoners. The hospital accommodation was good and the Japanese and their Manchurian lackeys had comfortable quarters. We met up with many of our friends from whom we had been parted months or even years ago and there was a lot of news to catch up. Our own conditions were better than we had had in previous camps; there was a large exercise yard and we were left pretty much to organise our own affairs. For some reason I had been made squad leader and had certain responsibilities but not many additional 'perks'. We spent much time cultivating our gardens and I managed to play a lot of bridge and poker – the latter against American colleagues, which certainly sharpened up my game. I had also volunteered to work in the hospital. Some years after my release I read that prisoners in this camp had been subjected to medical experiments by Japanese doctors. I saw no evidence of this while I was in the camp but cannot speak for what went on previously. Rumour had it that the camp was on American intelligence maps as an 'Aircraft assembly plant'. Certainly it had been bombed before we arrived, the high brick walls had been breached, a large hole had been created and the Japanese, so we were told, spent some time firing across the gap in case anyone tried to escape. Even in this remote part of the world, our captors still had this complex about people escaping. Just look at Mukden on a map. I suppose the nearest safe haven was the Russian Trans-Siberian Railway but that was a long way to travel. I never heard tell of anyone managing to escape in Manchuria.

From April 1945 until August, when we knew the war had ended, most of our time was spent attempting to keep fit mentally and physically. The Japanese had ceased to require us to work on menial tasks and most of the administration of the camp was in our hands. Our food was no better but it was different, with less reliance on rice. We did get some Red Cross parcels but not many and when the war ended considerable quantities of Red Cross stores were found in Japanese warehouses.

Chapter 13

Last Days of Captivity

Thousands of words have been written on the subject of the atomic bomb and even as I sit today in front of my word processor, the press are wondering whether Iraq has the bomb and whether it might use it. All war is dreadful and one wonders just how 'just' the Gulf conflict is; if it brings lasting peace to that cauldron it might have achieved some purpose.

My contribution to the debate on the atomic bomb is this: 'If the bomb had not been dropped on Japan, I am convinced that I would not be writing this.' By the beginning of August our Japanese guards who had relatives in Japan, were becoming increasingly twitchy about the effect of the bombings of their cities. It was not easy to get firm information from them but one guard told me that the fires in Tokyo had destroyed a large part of the capital. About this time, early August, we were told to prepare for a long march. As we would have to carry all our possessions we were warned to travel light. This caused great consternation in the camp as we knew exactly where we were and we could not imagine any destination – certainly not one that held out hope of long-term survival. Had the atomic bomb not been dropped, I do not know what would have happened to us but I am certain that prisoners of war would have suffered the ultimate penalty if the mainland of Japan had become a battlefield.

We, of course, had no knowledge of the fact that the Japanese establishment – with the exception of the hard core Army Generals – had decided that Japan could not win the war and the best chance they had of saving something from the mess was to sue for peace. I do not remember the exact date and I did not record it in my diary but it must have been about 10th August when a Manchurian guard in the hospital where I was working said, 'A large bomb has wiped out the whole of a Japanese town called Hiroshima.' My knowledge of the language was not extensive and I had always concentrated on learning such words of command as 'Move' and 'Fall in' on parade, so I questioned him at some length. He was adamant that one solitary bomb had caused all this destruction. I went back to our barracks and confided in a man for whom I had a lot of admiration. Colonel Ashton was a small, dark-haired character with a mild manner and a resilient sense of humour – he was also a very good bridge partner. He was a very senior officer in the Royal Army Ordnance Corps and when I told him this improbable tale he said, 'Perhaps they have succeeded in harnessing nuclear fission!!' I thought my scientific upbringing at Oxford had been pretty comprehensive but I admit to getting a lesson in atomic physics in darkest Manchuria. He was a man of great stature and a wonderful friend to me.

The second bomb was dropped on Nagasaki on 9th August, the day that Russia invaded Manchuria, and so entered the war against Japan. Both events had a dramatic effect on our situation. Soon we were told that there would be no long march and that we should remain within the camp perimeter.

Historians are of the opinion that the entry of Russia into the war, by their invasion of Manchuria, had a greater effect in persuading the Japanese that their cause was lost than had the dropping of the two atomic bombs. We, of course, were unaware of the diplomatic negotiations which had been taking place via Moscow and, after we learnt that Russia had entered the war, were mainly concerned with keeping our noses clean and a very low profile.

I had the misfortune to develop an abscess on one of my molars and the American dentist decided that an extraction was the only answer. He said that he had a very little of his precious store of anaesthetics left – I swear to this day that it must have been distilled water. It was very painful but, because of his skill, soon over.

Things really came to a head on 16th August when we saw a number of parachutes drop from a plane a mile or so from the camp. Although the camp was surrounded by high brick walls, we could see quite a lot of the surrounding countryside from the upper floors of our barracks. We had heard of the entry of Russia into the war and imagined that the parachute dropping was a Japanese practice, as the figures were too far away to identify. The drop took place in the morning; during the afternoon from a vantage point in the hospital I was able to see into the office of the Japanese Camp Commandant. There was an American officer still wearing his revolver and the Japanese had placed his sword on his desk. That seemed evidence enough to me that the war was over and I placed a few bets with my unconvinced colleagues. There was no great rejoicing – just a great sense of relief. The official announcement was not made to us until the morning of the 17th by the most senior officer in our camp. My feelings were expressed in the first letter I was able to write home.

Hoten Prisoner of War Camp,
Mukden.
19th August 1945

Dearest All,

This, I think, is the most difficult letter I have ever had to write. I have so much to tell you, so much to ask and so little time in which to write it.

You can imagine how I feel after three and a half years knowing that once more I am a free man with my own life to live. Many times during my captivity have I looked forward to the end and attempted to imagine the way in which the news would reach us. The actual story is like a modern thriller. We have had no official news issued to us since April 1943 but, because of the bravery of people working outside the camp, have never been far behind in the main world events. We knew of the entry of Russia into this war and were not surprised to see a number of parachutists descend from a plane on the morning of the 16th. Everybody, without exception, imagined it to be a Nipponese practice and we were amazed to see three Americans, one Jap and one Chinese arrive in the camp during the afternoon. Their treatment and reception led some of us to believe that the war must be over and, coupled with rumours from outside the camp, I was convinced. Some still remained unconvinced and I was able to remove a certain sum of money from my friends in bets. Our senior officer gave us the official announcement on the morning of the 17th. The atmosphere has been calm, unbelievably calm, and there have been no unpleasant incidents whatsoever, even though we are still guarded by the Nips. The internal administration is, however, in our hands. We are at the moment expecting a plane loaded with supplies and other things to make life more interesting. This letter will be flown away tomorrow with the sick in the camp and we expect to leave in about a week's time by ship. This, however, is mere conjecture since the airmen who arrived only managed to contact their Headquarters last night. They brought a small 1,000-

mile transmitter and today we hope for a more powerful set which will keep us in contact with the outside world.

The Russian troops have not yet entered the city or the outskirts where this camp is situated but we expect them within forty-eight hours. The Nips have been loath to surrender in this part of the world and some of us have been slightly apprehensive during the last few days.

I cannot give you anything but a rough idea of our treatment and conditions, it is sufficient to say that God has looked after me and I have just returned from giving thanks for his protection and blessing. I have been in this camp since April 1945 and it has been a period of comparative calm. Before that my moves were Changi: Singapore, February-August 1942; Heito: Taiwan, August 1942-August 1943; Shirakawa: Taiwan, August 1943-February 1945; then a sea voyage, the worst part of our captivity. Myata: Japan, March-April 1945, then here. We have been treated as criminals all the time and our status as officers has never been recognised. You probably know all this and I won't enlarge upon it, many of us died and I lost a number of friends on the wayside. I myself have had a few narrow escapes mainly due to disease but I'm through and that is all that matters.

In all I have had only sixty letters out of the many hundreds which I am sure must have been written to me; the last written by Mother in September 1944 I received in February 1945. Since then I have not heard a word. The facilities set up by the Nips for communication with our people have been almost useless and some men are waiting for their first letter. I have only heard of the arrival of one of the few I have written but hope you have fairly recent news of me.

Our food has been disgusting and, now that we have European food, many people are having stomach troubles. The Red Cross has been hindered in all its works and I personally have had not more than five food parcels in three and a half years. This, I think, can be taken as a general average, certainly for the people in Taiwan. Medical supplies have always been short and while I worked in the hospital in Shirakawa I saw many people die who could have been saved by adequate drugs alone. All this I am sure will be published and I warn you that most of the stories about Japanese atrocities can easily be believed.

This all sounds depressing and is in direct contradiction to the way that I feel. This afternoon I expect my own General will arrive. I was made A.D.C. to General Percival just before we surrendered and actually drove him out to that ceremony. He, together with Sir Shenton Thomas, has been separated from us for three years and we hope to see them today.

I know so little about you all that I can't say anything which will have any bearing on present doings. One thing, however, has always been uppermost in my mind, Hugh's safety and well being. I have never ceased to worry about him since I knew he had come out into this area. When I get news from you I hope to hear that he is safe and home. You can imagine my joy at Dad's new appointment and all the things that it means. What other members of our clan are doing I can't imagine. Marriage and perhaps births have entered the lists, I suppose, but I sincerely hope death has spared us for a great re-union.

That is all I can write now. I will attempt to compose a more cohesive screed to you whenever I have time, paper and sufficient time to think.

Love to all of you, broadcast the news to all my friends.

Your loving son.

I knew that my brother had come out to the east because of a coded message in one of the brief postcards my mother was able to send. 'Hugh will probably see the Meadens.' The Meadens were the couple who had been so kind to me when I called at Colombo, Ceylon, on my way out to Malaya. In fact, a gunner officer like me, he saw action in Burma.

I cannot add much to the story in my letters. It was a very exciting time but two events stand out in my memory. I had played a lot of poker in a school with American and British officers. So that we could keep some control over the game and stop extreme play, we always had a limit. The night that we knew we were free men, we sat down in our barracks wearing the traditional green eye-shades!! Someone suggested taking off the limit and I soon gave up my seat, pleading the need to 'spend a penny'. When I returned only two players were left, one an American Lieutenant from 'The Bronx' and the other a taciturn Colonel for whom I had a great respect. I was shattered to see that the stakes had risen to astronomical levels as both players were convinced they had the winning hand. Poker players will be interested to know how this situation had been reached. Both men had drawn two cards, the first had drawn the fourth Ace to the three he had been dealt. The other player had kept the Jack, ten and nine of hearts and he drew the Queen and the eight of the same suit to give him the winning hand. In the end, reason prevailed with a little help from the spectators and the stakes were set at half a year's pay! I remember the plaintive cry – leaving out the picturesque expletives – 'The first time in my life I have four aces and I — —— have to lose.'

The other story is a very sad event, I had become very friendly with an American sergeant called Jimmie Aulds who came from Louisiana. We were greatly outnumbered by the Americans and, while we found many of them very charming individually, *en masse* they tended to be a bit over-powering. There was always something in The States which was bigger, better or in some other way superior to anything we had to offer. Jimmie was a quiet, reserved character with a wonderful sense of humour. Before the land route had been established, large American transport planes flew near our camp and dropped supplies by parachute. We, of course, were delighted to see the stores, the like of which we had not seen for years. We gathered near the dropping zone so that we could quickly recover the packages and get them into our camp. Little did we appreciate the dangers until a net carrying cases of corned beef broke, scattering the boxes all over the place. One unfortunately hit Jimmy and he died before we could get him to the hospital. What a fate, having survived three and a half years as a prisoner.

My hopes of seeing General Percival again were dashed as he and other senior officers were flown to Chungking and did not come anywhere near our camp. They had been contacted by some of the Americans who para-chuted into Manchuria near our camp but it was some days later when some Russian troops were able to arrange overland transport to the airport near Mukden. General Percival, with General Wainwright, had been in-vited to attend the surrender ceremony in Tokyo Bay and they were flown there via Chungking and Manila. At one point I had outside hopes of being in the party but space on the aircraft was very limited and priority had to go to the very senior and the sick. General Percival was allowed to take his batman Sergeant Crockett, who had been with him the whole of his captiv-ity. No man set a better example of steadfastness under duress, he was al-ways smart and could put on a brave face in the most difficult of circum-stances. It was a fitting reward that he was to see the final acts of surrender.

We, after the announcement on the 17th that the war had ended, were in a state of limbo. The Japanese were still guarding the camp and, much as we might have wished to go outside the perimeter, it was clearly an unstable and possibly dangerous situation. So we waited for the arrival of the Russian troops and my next letter describes what happened. I had managed to get some rice paper and some ink but the paper was so thin that writing was difficult.

Hoten P.O.W. Camp
24th August 1945

Dearest All,

I write my letters to you without any specific addressee because I know you will pass them round the family. Paper, envelopes and time are all short so I hope you will share anything I send.

We are passing through a very exciting time here and the last few days have been so interesting that one is not quite as impatient as one was when we knew the war had ended.

I told you about the arrival of the intrepid parachute jumpers, they came without authority or command in a purely advisory and liaison capacity. When they arrived the Russian forces were still some distance away and it was not until the night of the 19th that the first Russian troops entered the town. A mission came into the camp immediately, led by a Captain on the Marshal's staff. He had met the American Ninth Army in Berlin and then made a promise to do all he could to release prisoners in this part of the world. He was most excited and said it was one of the happiest moments of his life to tell us that we were free men. Until then we had been under the Nip administration and for their edification and instruction he lined up the whole camp staff in front of us. There followed a ceremony which I never expected to see.

This camp contains about 1,750 people, of whom over 1,200 are American; it also contains all the Allied Senior Officers of the rank of full Colonel and above except the Governors and heads of Armies like General Wainwright and General Percival. We are housed in huge barracks three in number, outside is a huge exercise yard in which air-raid trenches have been dug. The Russian lined up all the Nip officers, nine in number, and the guard consisting of about thirty N.C.O.s and men. Their arms and equipment were piled in front of them and the American officer of the guard was given an automatic pistol. He then ordered the guard to march the Nips off into confinement. He then told the senior officer, American Maj. Gen. Parker, that everything in the camp, including the Nips, belonged to us. While the Nips were being marched off there was no demonstration and everything was done in an orderly fashion. I expected to see some attempted action against the dozen or so 'bad ones' in the camp but everything was kept well under control. The next morning, instead of the Nips ordering the prisoners about, they themselves were under guard cleaning out the drains and doing other menial duties.

Only yesterday did the Russians send in enough troops to control the Town and in the morning we received a visit from the Commander in this area and his staff. They have put up a most magnificent show in this campaign and they themselves are as pleased with their success as they were in Germany. They had a girl with them who spoke excellent English as well as eight other languages.

The gates have been opened for the first time today but the town is still out of bounds. Some men, of course, have been out and have returned in an extremely intoxicated condition. There has been quite a lot of fighting between the Chinese and the Japs. The latter are fighting a losing battle because both our people and the Russians disarm the Japs and immediately give the arms to the Chinese. I hope to be able to go into the town in a few days and there is talk of establishing a guard house there if we are here for any length of time. Money is very little use to us but any spare clothes are fetching a high price with the Chinese. About all we can buy are fruit and eggs. Liquor is finding its way past the guard house and yesterday I had my first drink for years – it tasted like fire water.

I don't know when I shall be home. We managed to 'get' a wireless set and, after rewinding the coils, received London. Just as we got the King's speech the power went off so we do not know what he said. We gather, however, the prisoners from the East are No. 1 priority and everyone hopes that we may fly home. At present the plan is to fly us to Manila and then perhaps to India. Originally we were supposed to go to Chungking. Nothing is likely to happen until MacArthur occupies Japan. We have had three planes in here and today I smoked my first fresh cigarette for many months. The first plane left this morning after bursting a tyre and I hope it carried my first letter to you. The planes are B24s and I gather that the aerodrome is not big enough to take them in large numbers. The one which arrived yesterday was flown by a Captain Hillsman, U.S.A.C., whose father, a Colonel, is a prisoner in this camp. The old man was frightfully bucked and his son is waiting for some time before returning. He holds a position on the War Guilt Tribunal which is operating in this area.

We have been having some good food lately and I am very much fitter. It will shock you to know that my average weight over the last two years has been about 8 st. 5 lb., not much but not as light as some people. This morning I had an unfortunate tussle with the camp dentist and he scored an overwhelming victory. I lost one of my prized grinders in a hectic five-minute round. The Japanese anaesthetic did not work and when the crown snapped off in the first minute my troubles really started. However, he was quick and I am now recovering in a drugged haze. This is the only tooth I have lost but it will take about ten visits to get everything put straight.

I will write again soon and send you numerous cables once we start. The main thing in my mind at the moment is the location of my family and I will try to let you have an address so you can let me know where you are. One thing I feel certain about is that my dear Aunt Sadie will still have a 'boys' room' and, as our American friends say, 'Boy, believe you me after two years on a floor it will be marvellous.'

All love to everyone.

Our stay in Mukden was much longer than we anticipated and all notions of being flown home quickly soon went out of the window. We settled to a new sort of life and for a spell I was made a liaison officer with the Russian Headquarters. I never knew how this happened except that I had a smattering of Japanese and was a squad leader. The job did not amount to much but I was able to get a prime position for the Victory Parade which the Russians put on.

There was a large impressive building in the middle of the town with a large raised terrace on the front of the building. Steps lead down to street level. Two main roads emanate from the building rather like spokes in a huge wheel. The plan was that the Russian troops would parade down one of the streets, pass the saluting base and disappear up the other street. Tanks were mixed with armoured personnel carriers, lorries and staff cars. We could see the parade start but gradually mechanical failure took its toll and there were more gaps than vehicles when they reached the saluting base.

Gradually we became more adventurous and ventured into the town of Mukden. We had been warned about the Russian troops and were very careful when we met them. We had one nasty experience when some Russians fought with some of our people and removed watches and other valuables. The section responsible was identified by their badges and quite horrific punishment meted out to them.

We managed to track down a distillery and saw a familiar square bottle with a red label and the legend 'Guaranteed twelve DAYS old' and it certainly tasted like it. Some people, ignoring the advice of our doctors, took rather too much on board and were seriously ill. We took good care to be back in our camp well before nightfall.

As the days passed, we got more and more frustrated because of lack of news and lack of action about our move home. We were dependent on the Russians because it was clear that air evacuation of the numbers involved was not possible. However, it became clear that the Russians were much more interested in getting anything that could be moved out of Manchuria and back to Russia. Machine tools, cars, lorries, etc., etc., were loaded onto rail wagons and moved westwards. Our conditions and, of course, our food were greatly improved but that did not stop us hoping for a sign that things were happening. My next letter to my parents expressed some of that frustration.

29th August 1945

My dear Mother and Father,

I am writing this letter to you both but some of the contents may interest other people. I hope you will tell them if anything can be passed on.

It is fairly difficult to write to you because I have had no news from you for about a year and cannot imagine what things are like at home. I don't even know if either of you are in England. As far as I can see I shall have little opportunity of finding out until I actually arrive home as there cannot be much chance of in-coming mail here. The plans for our evacuation seem to have come to a full-stop at the moment and we cannot get any information whatsoever. I suppose about sixty people, including the very sick and the very senior officers, have been flown to Chungking but my news about our going is merely rumour. Something of which we have had more than enough during our captivity.

At the moment we await the arrival of an American Process Group whose exact function is unknown but supposed to be the administration of evacuation from here. Their arrival has been delayed by bad weather in this area and they may not be here until tomorrow. The Americans made a fine show landing here by parachute at the time of the surrender but since then have done nothing except talk. We have had so much bombastic drivel from them whilst we have lived in the same camp. Now some sample of their boasted efficiency and drive would be very welcome.

I am unable to make any plans here. What my position is within the Colonial Office I don't know. Few people in the Malayan Civil Service got away and I hope they will want me back in the country fairly quickly. Many of the senior people in the service have been killed and many more died in captivity. Some of the older men who have been interned will, I am sure, never return to the country. The civilian internees were in Changi Gaol in Singapore and when we left in August 1942 conditions were not good. Sir Shenton Thomas, the Governor of Singapore, has been with our senior generals all the time and is pretty fit at the moment.

I hope that I will be demobilised pretty quickly and will not hesitate to call on General Percival to help me if I think he can be of any assistance. He promised that he would do all he could in that way when I left him in Formosa.

I am getting very bored in this place and longing for the day when we start for home. Everyone has been looking forward to seeing their loved ones again and this period seems to be the longest of our captivity. If only we could start moving everyone would be so much happier. We are allowed out but the town is about seven miles away and the glamour of newly released prisoners has begun to wear off with the Russians who have a job of work to do. They showed commendable hospitality during the first few days after our release but now one gets quite a cool reception in Russian H.Q. The funniest thing lately has been our exchange market. We have no money and the local inhabitants have no clothes, we have exchanged everything under the sun from socks to black-out curtains.

The currency in the place is the Yen or Yuan but it is worth practically nothing. A year ago an egg cost ten sen, now it costs 500 times that price. Any money which we get is immediately converted into more tangible assets such as condensed milk and eggs. The first people out in the morning send back a report on the state of the market so that others following can decide what part of their wardrobe must be sacrificed for the day's entertainment. I append a specimen:-

1 blanket (not new)	= Yuan 12	= 22 eggs
1 pr warm underpants	= Yuan 80	= 1 tin milk
		(difficult, he wanted 100)
1 pr new Jap socks	= Yuan 20	= 1 watermelon
(from store in camp)		(market unstable, also fruit)

You can see that we have some amusing moments trying to decide whether six eggs in the stomach are better than a vest outside it. One sees anyone from a Private to a Brigadier going out with his bankroll over his arm and returning with his hat full of eggs. I have been feeding well, having a personal servant who knows the head storeman well, and have put on pounds in the last fourteen days.

A brewery which was Japanese controlled was found in the town and after two people established that the Russians did not object to cases being removed the news spread. People landed in the camp with trucks, carts and bicycles laden with cases of the stuff. There are forty-eight junior officers in our section commanded by self, but that story comes later, and we drank about thirty cases of twenty-four bottles in three days. Everybody thought that the first smell would be sufficient to render anyone intoxicated. It is untrue; in one night I drank seven bottles and the only effect it had was to increase firing time from once to four. The Russians finally got annoyed and published an order that no more beer should be removed, before informing us that they had shot the horses of five carts and taken a pot shot at the owners. We have a certain amount in store and I can hardly get into my bed for the stuff.

I've just seen an American plane arriving so perhaps things are happening. I am perpetually questioned by my squad about the beastly things and can never give an answer. As I said, I am in charge of forty-eight junior officers. All except four are older than I am, and about ten are senior by appointment. However, I stand no nonsense and there is a fine spirit of co-operation which has always distinguished the British sections.

That I am afraid must be all.

Every day seems to pass very slowly. I long for the day when I will see you again.

Your loving son.

We were, of course, just itching to start on our journey home and the days passed very slowly. We devised all sorts of interests to try to occupy the time. The administration of the camp had been taken over by an American Colonel Donovan who flew in from Chungking – a man for whom I developed the greatest admiration.

He held regular briefing meetings with the squad leaders, giving us as much information as possible, On the one hand he had all of us pressing for action and on the other hand the Russians, who appeared to us to be very dilatory in arranging transport for us. He walked this tight-rope with great skill.

There were some amusing incidents. I was still working in the hospital and one morning one of our number came in complaining of severe pains in his ribs. The doctor diagnosed a cracked rib and asked how it had happened. Our hero said that he had tripped and fallen against a kerb-stone. 'How,' asked the doctor, 'was the bruising all round your rib-cage and not on one side only?' After a lot of questioning, countered by evasive answers, it transpired that the victim had met a Russian Sergeant Major (female) and had been invited back to her quarters for a drink. Things clearly went from good to better and an embrace resulted in the damage. Poor hero had to retreat with 'mission unaccomplished'!

My feelings about having to hang on in Mukden instead of setting off for home were expressed in a letter I wrote to my mother.

> Mukden Prisoner of War Camp,
> Manchuria.
> 8th September 1945

My dear Mother,

At one time I hoped to be home for your birthday (22nd Sept.). That is impossible and once again I must send you my dearest love and best wishes instead of being able to give you them in person. I do hope you have a happy birthday.

The news of our evacuation is getting 'hot'; today we heard that units of the American Seventh Fleet had arrived in Daeren to take us away. Col. Donovan who is in charge here now, having come from Chungking, has gone to that port to see if he can arrange transport for us with the Russians. If anyone can do it, he can. No matter how far the American High Command looked, I'm sure they could not find a better man to send here. He's tall, good-looking, shy and retiring but when anything has to be done he moves everything. I should hate to be on the mat in front of him. Where we shall go from here I cannot imagine but if I see a chance of going home by the States I will try to wangle it. I have been in camps with Americans throughout my captivity and have many fine friends amongst them.

To divert to a more serious topic; I have written to the Colonial Office telling them I expect to be repatriated in the near future and that I shall communicate with them at the earliest opportunity. I should be very grateful if you could find out what they intend to do with me. A spot of leave would be very useful and I think I deserve it, even if am at the bottom of the leave roster. Perhaps you or Dad, who knows everybody there, could get the wheels turning to ensure my early demobilisation. The Army will never do that quickly unless some pressure can be brought to bear. You will, I am sure, realise that I am very helpless here and I know you will do all you can.

The matter of Pay and Allowances must wait until I return. I think I am on sufficiently intimate terms with all the senior officers in Malaya Command, from General Percival downwards, to get that straightened out.

I must push this into the post now. I've got lots to tell you but it can wait until I see you.

Very best love to you all and, again, best wishes for your birthday.

Your loving son.

It was marvellous to know that, once again, we could write letters that would get home in pretty quick time. The American Army postal services gave top priority to letters with the legend 'Liberated U.K. P.W. Officer'.

Preparations went ahead for our departure from Manchuria and I recall the immunisation programme for typhus, plague, cholera, triple typhoid and smallpox. The American doctors put all 1,700 of us past four 'syringe merchants' like sheep through a gate. We got two jabs at a time, one in each arm, and felt like a pincushion at the end of it all.

We had been out of touch with the world for so long that there were great gaps in our knowledge of the way the war had developed. Every evening in the camp we had a cinema show with all the latest films from America. Before the show Col. Donovan gave us the latest news about the prospects for our journey home, always a popular act, and a Sergeant Fred Friendly, who was a reporter on the Colonel's staff, talked for an hour to bring us up to date. He had been in many battle areas and was quite brilliant in choosing just the right subjects for our education. All this made the time pass more quickly but it seemed a very long time to wait.

We spent most of our time within the camp perimeter. The thrill of swapping vests for eggs soon paled and we were increasingly wary of problems with the Russian troops. Food supplies were more than adequate so there was not the need to get local goods.

Chapter 14

On Our Way

At last the news came that we were to start on our journey home, and no news has ever been received with greater joy. It had seemed a long time to be hanging about in Mukden but everything possible was being done for us. As the Russians seemed to be concentrating on removing anything of value from Manchuria to the homeland, it was not surprising that our affairs had such a low priority.

Then we were off by train to the Manchurian port of Daeren or Port Arthur. The journey was comfortable, we would have thought that cattle trucks were acceptable so long as we were moving in the right direction. On 12 September, almost a month after we knew we were free men, we joined the U.S. Hospital Ship *Relief*. What a joy it was to sleep in clean bedclothes on a reasonably soft mattress after the straw mattresses and pillows which had served us for three and a half years. It was so comfortable that many of us had difficulty in getting to sleep. The crew were marvellous and we got a great welcome from them.

Our troubles were by no means over as the waters through which we sailed were still liable to have mines floating about. We had a strong escort of American warships and they exploded four mines on our voyage to Okinawa; it was an impressive sight to see the huge geyser of water as the mine was hit by machine-gun fire. We learnt later that the cruiser *Louisville*, which was following us with more prisoners of war, had hit a mine and two of the crew had been killed. How wrong it seemed for men to survive the hazards of years of combat and then to die so soon after the end of hostilities.

When we arrived off Okinawa and were preparing to disembark our passengers, we were warned that a typhoon was heading in our direction and we were ordered to go to sea and take shelter behind the island.

We had already seen the American Fleet at anchor and that too was ordered to sail; it was a most impressive sight. There followed a really frightening twenty-four hours as we rode the storm about seventy miles from the island of Okinawa. The ship pitched and rolled and most people were very sea-sick; the ship rolled very close to its maxi-mum and seemed to take ages to roll back to the vertical before pitching and rolling to the other side. We were told that we were some distance from the centre of the storm but I could not really imagine any worse weather. All moveable objects had to be lashed down and we moved from one place to the next with great caution, holding onto anything within our grasp. It was impossible for the galley to prepare food and we managed on 'iron rations' which, for us, was as good as anything we had tasted for years.

After what seemed an age the storm abated and we anchored in a huge bay and were taken ashore. We couldn't believe our eyes when we saw the warships of all shapes and sizes lined up as far as the eye could see. While we were sorry to say goodbye to the crew of the hospital ship, we were glad to get our feet on dry land again.

We spent one night in a camp on Okinawa and then were off again to fly to the Philippines but we were treated to an open-air concert soon after we arrived. It was a little disconcerting to hear machine-gun firing half-way through the performance and the audience took cover at panic stations. It transpired that two Japanese, who had been hiding in a cave and did not know the war was over, decided to take offensive action. Fortunately no-one was seriously hurt.

The next morning we were driven to an airport and detailed to one of a number of B-24s, one of the smaller of America's four-engined bombers. Soon we had an example of the power of America's economic might; our plane had a radio which developed a fault. I'm sure the reaction of our services would be to change the radio and to delay take-off until it had been fixed. The Americans just called up another aircraft, loaded everyone onto it and we were off within minutes.

I had a wonderful seat where the navigator usually sat; he was sharing a desk with the radio operator so that they could take the maximum number of passengers. The weather was perfect and all seemed to be going to plan until we approached the northern island of Luzon; here a rapidly developing tropical storm forced us to land as quickly as possible. The pilot made a superb touch-down on a fighter strip, the runway was just about as wide as his wing-span. It was sometime later that we realised how close to real danger we had been and what a magnificent job the pilot had done. We spent the night in that small fighter station and were entertained right royally.

The next day we had the choice of another trip in the B-24 or 'chickening out' and going to Clarke Field, the big American air force base, overland. It was pretty rugged country and most people chose to stay with our intrepid crew. Very soon we had doubts as to whether this had been the correct decision. The strip on which we had landed was built on the top of some cliffs and the take-off was towards the sea. When we saw it in the cold light of day, it did seem a very small bit of tarmac but the Captain remained supremely confident. He stood on the brakes, opened the throttles and we roared along the run-way towards the cliff edge. When we cleared the edge, the plane did not climb immediately but descended ever so slowly towards the sea. I don't think I have ever prayed so hard before or since; we could not have been more than fifty feet above the water when we levelled out and then started to climb. We breathed a sigh of relief and gave vent to a muffled cheer. We arrived safely at Clarke Field and changed planes to a C47 – the famous Dakota work-horse – for our last 150 kilometres to Manila. Even then our troubles were not over. A plane had crashed on the runway and it was two hours before the wreckage could be cleared and we could land. Fortunately we had enough fuel but the pilot assured us that there were other diversionary airfields if we had to abandon Manila. In forty-eight hours I had just about as much excitement as my frail body could take.

I summed up all this in a letter I wrote to my mother as soon as we had settled in at our new camp. This was outside the city of Manila and run by the Americans with some help from Australian forces. It was the staging post for British and Australian troops; very comfortable and the food was excellent but soon the old impatience to be on the move reared its ugly head.

Manila.
22 September 1945

My dear Mother,

I write this to you on your birthday and hope the best present I can give you is the news that I am on my way home. When I return we must have a fine party, I don't think it will be long now. Wherever I am I will send you a cable; all, I'm glad to say, at the expense of Uncle Sam or John Bull. These will probably have a return address on them but don't write too much as it is quite likely I will not be able to collect them. There is some mail in the camp now, written sometime after the war ended and I hope to be able to collect some today; the sorting, of course, takes some time.

Our journey up to the present has been quick and comfortable. I'll only tell you the bare facts, the details and the stories can wait until I see you. We left Daeren on the 12th in the U.S. hospital Ship *Relief* and sailed for Okinawa. The escort vessels with us exploded four mines on the way down and you will have heard that the cruiser *Louisville* which followed with more ex-prisoners on board struck one. Fortunately there were no casualties amongst the passengers but two of the crew were killed. What rotten luck to go through the war and then be killed so soon after peace came. When we arrived off Okinawa a typhoon was reported and once again we had to go to sea. It was pretty rough but we were some distance from the centre and rode the storm about seventy miles from the island.

We went to a camp and after a night's sleep were driven to an airport and got into a B-24, one of the smaller four-engined bombers. I had a wonderful trip on the flight deck in the navigator's seat. He worked on the radio operator's table, he in his turn was doing his work on the deck. The weather was perfect and we sailed along at nearly 200 m.p.h. until we got to the north of Luzon. Here a tropical storm forced us down on a very small airfield. The pilot made a perfect landing even though the strip was hardly as wide as the wing-span of the plane. We spent the night of the 19th there and then flew to Clarke Field the next day. There we changed to a C-47 and came the 150 kilometres to Manila. We circled here for nearly two hours because of a crash on the airfield but finally got down and were brought to the camp. Everybody is very kind to us and the crews of the aircraft were magnificent. We are being processed and medically examined here and as soon as that's over we are ready to go. I think we shall go by ship, probably one of the aircraft carriers of the fleet out here.

The night we arrived here we saw Gracie Fields in person; she's getting very hard and has lost some of her spontaneity. Beer and gin come to us with regularity here and I'm once again feeling a free man.

I'll send you news all the way along. Don't bother to write unless you know there is a good chance of my getting the letter. It won't be long before I see you.

All my love.

The day after I wrote that letter I was delighted to receive one from my Uncle, giving me a wonderful summary of all that had happened to members of the family since I had been captured. Thomas Munro Simpson had married my father's sister and while my parents were abroad had been like a father to my brother and myself. We were brought up with our three girl cousins in their lovely country home at Hepscott in Northumberland. My Uncle had inherited a major shareholding in the manufacturing chemists business Wilkinson & Simpson Ltd. He had qualified as a pharmacist and for most of the time that I knew him he was Managing Director of the company. I always feel that he would have been happier looking after the family farms, as he was a skilled gardener, and I spent many hours with him building bridges and lily ponds. He left his estate in trust for his wife and then his daughters and I hope that I am repaying some of his great kindness to me by acting as a Trustee.

My uncle had seen an address in the press to which he could write and had sat down immediately to give me this wonderful synopsis of all that had happened in the family. I was particularly delighted to hear that my mother had been able to join my father in Nigeria and that my brother was safe after serving in Burma.

We were gradually regaining our strength on the good food and drink and the Americans were most generous in the matter of new clothes. We had no access to our own uniforms but I managed to get a wonderful selection of American officers' light-weight jackets and trousers. I also acquired a sort of bomber jacket which was rather like a poacher's coat and had huge pockets both inside and out. I treasured it and wore it for years after I got home.

Although the camp was pleasant and everything possible was done to keep us amused, we became very impatient about the fact that we were not making any progress towards the U.K. In retrospect, I suppose we were being a little unfair as it was a massive task to move everyone to Australia and the U.K.; coming the other way were all the American troops from Europe. An extraordinary thing happened in our camp. We were visited by Lady Louis Mountbatten in her role as head of the Red Cross. I was wandering about dressed only in a pair of shorts and she stopped and asked me how I was getting on. I replied that we had no complaints about our treatment which was quite excellent but our only gripe was the speed at which we were getting home. Very few drafts seemed to be going to the U.K. and it seemed to us that the Australians were getting priority because their Government was making more song and dance than ours. She replied that her husband was not in overall command; had he been, he might have been able to do something about it. Two years later, at a dinner in Delhi at the Viceroy's Residence, Lady Louis said, 'I remember you, I think it was Manila and you were not dressed in a dinner jacket.' That was a marvellous feat of memory because she could not have been primed by one of her many A.D.C.s. But we became increasingly frustrated as another day passed without news of our departure across the Pacific.

I knew that my father had been made Chief Commissioner of the Northern Provinces of Nigeria and that my mother had joined him in Kaduna. I was hoping that perhaps I might be able to wangle my way home via Nigeria but this was not to be as it was too far off the track. I wrote to my parents almost every day.

28th September 1945

Dearest Both,

I write to you in an impatient mood. I've just missed two ships for home and am now first on the list in this camp. There are rumours of ships arriving but there is nothing definite yet. Some say the next one will go home by India, if so I shall not be there. I have absolutely no desire to go that way and it seems a pity to miss going across the American continent when I've got this far.

There is nothing to do here during the day and I spend most of my time on my back. We see a reasonable show each evening but even this cannot take one's mind off the homeward trip.

Postal arrangements leave much to be desired and the whole administration handling our evacuation is a very makeshift affair. My main consideration at the moment is clothes. I have some beautiful suits of American sun-tan uniforms which will be very useful in Malaya. I can't, however, see myself walking about in England in November wearing them. I hope we can get some warm uniforms before we arrive home. Perhaps arrangements have been made in America for its distribution.

Archie Bevan, a friend of mine in the Guards, went home yesterday via San Francisco. I've asked him to get in touch with Uncle Munro when he gets home and this will give them some idea about my time of arrival.

I hope for some news of going away soon. When it comes I'll try to raise the money to cable you, until then
        All my love.

And then another letter the next day:

Manila.
29th September 1945

Dearest Both,

I write to you both in Africa because I don't know if mother has moved homewards. Dad, I know, will send letters on as soon as possible.

There is much unrest in the camp at the moment and everyone is very bad-tempered. It all arises from the extreme slowness and inefficiency with which our evacuation is being carried out. We were all led to believe that once we had reached Manila all would be easy. The American Air Force got us here in grand style but since then absolutely nothing has been done. The camp is run by Australian officers and we have been deluged with Australian newspapers. These carry long articles about the slow release of Australian ex-P.O.W.s from this area and state that there are now 2,000 'held' in Manila.

The fact that there are 3,000 waiting to travel to the U.K., a journey three times as long, is of course not mentioned. All our senior officers are already on the way home and we are the poor orphans whom nobody loves. We are heartily disgusted with the whole affair and the visit of Admiral Sir Bruce Fraser gave us no encouragement whatsoever. He had been based in Australia for some time and when he spoke to us he seemed to be under the impression that there were only Australian officers present. Actually, the proportion is about one in ten. Two aircraft carriers are due and both are expected to go to Australia, obviously in an attempt to quell the Press uprising. When they have left there is a chance we shall start our journey home.

Changing the subject to pleasanter topics, I had drinks this morning with a lovely girl who had been in England exactly three weeks ago. She's a Lieutenant in the Red Cross Headquarters and talking to her was like a dose of tonic. Everything we read here is published outside England and tends to accentuate the difficult conditions at home. She, however, explained it all and the reports, giving the basic facts, give one a very distorted picture of actual conditions. She had a marvellous trip here by air – London, Cairo, Truk, Karachi, Colombo, Sydney, Cocos Islands and Manila.

They expect to remain here about six months and, of course, hope to go home by America to complete a 'round the world trip'. These girls are doing a wonderful job here, standing on their feet serving drinks for seven hours is not easy. The girl in question had never been out of England before and was thrilled with what she had seen.

It is hard to fill in one's day here but nearby is an airstrip run by the American Air Force. They take us up any time in these little cubs and we have great fun. They are very safe and fly close enough to the ground for one to see everything. I like the Americans very much; they have treated us magnificently since we were released and I have the highest respect for their lack of red tape, with the efficiency it seems to bring in all their services. Responsibility is shouldered by very junior officers who are never afraid to 'go on ahead'. One has only to mention the magic combination ex-P.O.W. and they will do anything – free beer, air trips – and to-night I'm having a party with two young air force colonels. I met them quite by chance but soon they had everything arranged for me.

We have some officers here who volunteered to come out and help us when they themselves had just been released from German Prison Camps. One was with his family within five days of release. It makes us feel very bad. One told me this morning that all the camps in which he stayed in Germany were better than the place in which we are now staying.

This is a grousing letter; there is nothing I like better than a legitimate grouse and this as our American friends say, 'is it'. I think it is all because we're more homesick than we have ever been before. Home seems so near and yet so far away and every day seems like a week.

I have had no news since uncle's fine letter but hope every day that something may arrive. As I told you, postal arrangements leave a lot to be desired but there are signs of reorganisation consequent upon the Press outcry from Australia.

I'm not really as depressed as I sound and look forward very much to seeing all the people about whom I have thought so much during the difficult months, forty-two in all.

Goodbye for now, I'll write again soon.

Your loving son.

Another week passed and I was still 'holed up' in Manila but I had soon adopted a more realistic approach to matters and decided to enjoy myself if at all possible. Female company was a wonderful help to greater confidence in the future, the Red Cross girls certainly helped us on our recovery process.

Just how true the following story is I do not know but was alleged to concern my great friend Flight Lieutenant 'Spud' Spurgeon R.A.A.F. In Manila the Americans, who had so much equipment the mind boggled, made everyone very welcome. There was a marked lack of red tape and soon the Australian pilots were allowed to fly some of the small communications aircraft. We were often taken for a spin and the views were outstanding as we flew over the harbour which was absolutely packed with ships of all shapes and sizes.

As one of the aircraft-carriers set sail, a small plane appeared over the flight deck, waggled its wings as though it was in distress and managed to touch down without incident. An irate flight deck officer dashed forward and yelled, 'Where the hell do you think you're going?' to which Spud replied, 'I hope we are both going to Australia, if so could you stow my aircraft below until we arrive.' I do not know the end of the story but I'm sure the Americans had so many planes they would not miss one little one.

More days passed, October arrived and on the 5th of the month I wrote to my parents.

> Just a line to let you know I'm still here and see no chance of moving for some days. British ships are doing a great job transporting Americans, Dutch and Australians but why not us? We've had a pretty raw deal and shall not hesitate to make it known should the opportunity arise.
>
> I'm having a great time here with a man called David Woodrow who rowed for Trinity when I was at New College. We've met some English girls in the Red Cross and they have a swimming pool. Having a particular girl friend on each shift means we can swim morning and afternoon. The camp has lost its dismal atmosphere. The fact that the barman is a 'Geordie' from Gateshead allows us to laugh at the camp ration. A certain amount of finesse is needed but I have three and a half years training in concealment and subsequent removal of illicit stores. We've repaired their fridge for them this morning so all the beer is iced now.
>
> I feel much fitter and the swimming is hardening my muscles. It is very hot here and malaria used to be a great menace; however,

the camp is sprayed regularly with D.D.T. from C-47s and I have never seen a mosquito.

Had a cable from Uncle Munro which told me he had had some news since I was free. He confirmed everything in his letter, which I gather was written 'on spec'. 'Hugh safe India' meant more to me than I can tell.

See you soon. They can't keep me here forever.

And indeed they could not because four days later on 9th October I was able to write:

I'm off today on the U.S. *Marine Shark* bound for San Francisco. She is a new 15,000-ton transport taking 1,100 troops so we should be quite comfortable.

I've had a wonderful time here lately, picnics, dances and swimming parties. The cause of it all was a lovely Red Cross Officer from England. She's a grand girl but that is another story and I am still fancy free.

I write this just before we board. See you soon, sorry it is so short.

Your loving son.

I don't know why it was but I seemed to be nominated for a number of administrative roles. I had been squad leader in Mukden and in Taiwan an assistant to the senior officer in the camp. This time I was made responsible for the 'pay and rations' of the British contingent on board the *Marine Shark* with instructions to keep a sharp eye on them and get them all home. This was a pretty formidable task and I think only three or four failed to make it to the U.K. I think some of the temptations along the way were too attractive to resist.

After all these years, nothing that I can remember describes our time on the *Marine Shark* as well as the letters I wrote home. It was a new troop transport, wonderfully fitted out and we saw the fulfilment of our wish that we should go home by the U.S.A.

At Sea.
14th October 1945

Dearest Both,
At last we are on our way home aboard the U.S.S. *Marine*

Shark, a 17,000-ton troop transport making her maiden voyage. It's a lovely ship, capable of eighteen knots, the speed it has been holding now for three days. The officers have plenty of space with nine to a stateroom in three-tier bunks. I have the top one with a fan at my head, beautiful clean sheets awaited us and we are really very comfortable. The food is excellent and the joy of having china and cutlery again is one of the greatest things about being free. Our table steward is a youngster who is proud of his efficiency and we do very well. Ice-cream comes to us at least once a day and fresh milk for the first time in over four years has a taste of its own. The only drawback is the queer regulation about drink, all American ships are dry and I do like one before dinner.

We are making for Hawaii now on the southern route, having passed Guam two days ago. The Captain decided to take the southern passage because he thought a too rapid change to cold weather would have an unwelcome effect upon our health. We are deeply grateful because it means there is less chance of going to Vancouver and it makes a trip to San Francisco more probable. If we continue to make the same mileage each day as we have done up to the moment, we shall arrive the day before Navy Day, when all the U.S. Fleet which can be spared will be in San Francisco harbour. I think we should have a good time. The Americans have been wonderful to us and have done everything to make this trip home something we shall always remember.

I don't know whether you have read about a figure in this theatre of war called Major Arthur Weirmuth, the 'one man army of Bataan'. He's a great friend of mine and we hope to have some fun when we arrive in San Francisco. A big reception has been planned for him and we shall probably come in for some of the entertainment. It is a funny thing but many of our officers find it difficult to get on with the Americans. I like them and their conversation amuses me. They are difficult to understand and have a very different code of manners and morals to ours. There are some American nurses on board and some of them are good fun. They have done a magnificent job in this part of the world and are going home to a well-earned rest. The conditions under which they have lived and worked have been as bad as the combat troops. They have a fine record, 98.6 per cent of all their wounded survived.

The weather has been beautiful on this trip so far, sunny and a lovely breeze. I'm trying to keep a nice coat of suntan until I get home. Unfortunately it is fading now and I must step up the dose. We have a sun deck reserved for officers and nurses and it is a very comfortable spot.

You will realise that this is being written in patches but that is the only way on a ship. I am paymaster for our officers and men, 1,600 in all, and it takes quite a bit of time. My accounts for the $20,000 are straight now and I hope and pray they will remain so throughout the voyage. The British Government are keeping us very short of money. I only hope I may be able to get some in the States or Canada, wherever we go. I want to buy some presents for Mother and the girls, I believe perfume and stockings can be had now.

17 October 1945

The statement which I made earlier to the effect that there is no drink on the ship is incorrect. I met the ship's surgeon, a young major, two nights ago and he invited me to a small party. We had an excellent evening and I was on my best behaviour. Being the only Englishman present laid me open to a good deal of good-natured chaffing. Some of the people had never really talked to any of us before and after a while said that we weren't so different after all. The surgeon is a nice fellow but very conceited; unfortunately he's one of those people who can't talk about anything except his own job.

We are still making good time and expect to arrive in Hawaii in four days time. We have two Thursdays this week so I make a day. The weather is beautiful and I spend most of my days in the sun. I've got a lovely mahogany tan and hope it remains until I get home amongst the pale-faces.

I've written to brother Hugh for his twenty-first birthday and hope I can see him so I can give him something he wants. I feel I know so little about him now, Cambridge, the Army, action, and all that that means, must have changed him considerably. I know that he will be the same lovable Hugh and I feel sure that if our leaves coincide, we can all have some good times together. I have asked him to write and tell me all about himself and look forward to a lot of letters when I get to Hepscott [the home of my Uncle Munro].

18 October 1945

We have had a little set-back these last few days, a bearing has been heating up and we are losing about seventy miles a day. The weather yesterday was unpleasant, a head sea, rain and a high wind. It wasn't very cold but I do like the sun.

My job as paymaster has suffered a severe reverse, the Commander of all the troops who had my money in his safe had a bad heart attack two days ago and has been in no condition to reveal the combination of the safe. I wish I could get the job finished and all my accounts straight.

19th October 1945

Another lovely day but the ship is running slower than ever, the bearing seems to be heating up more and more and the speed can't be much over ten knots. We may have to put in for repairs in Hawaii and if so I must try to bathe on Wakiki beach. It would be a pity to land there and not visit that technicolour spot.

I hope to complete my pay-roll today. Unfortunately when we started paying this morning, the ship's officers decided to search the ship for ammunition. Some of the men have been taking 20 mm shells and they are highly dangerous. Some of them do the most stupid things but on the whole they are very well behaved.

I'm posting this in Hawaii tomorrow where we expect to stop for about two days for repairs. There is no news about shore leave but we hope to see some of the place. Five days away is 'Frisco and then some story about going home by Canada. I do so want to see America and I'll be very disappointed if we go the northern route. I shall also be very cold.

Love to you both.

We were disappointed that we were not allowed ashore in Hawaii, from our vantage point it appeared to be a wonderful place. I suppose the authorities were afraid that, once we had been allowed ashore, they would have problems getting us on board again. I think this was all tied in with the belief, not outwardly expressed but suspected, that the returning prisoners of war might not be entirely sane – and certainly could not be trusted. This was a most monstrous criticism, we might not have been in the greatest shape physically but those who survived were very resilient mentally.

The next stages of my journey home were pretty chaotic and my letters covered a week or more. I can do no better than repeat the letters and then fill in the gaps.

At Sea.
30th October 1945

We are still on this old ship and expect to reach San Francisco tomorrow and perhaps disembark the day after. This is a trip I will always remember, the only thing the ship has not managed to do is SINK. We went into Hawaii but were not allowed ashore; the place is beautiful and we docked in Pearl Harbour. The night after we left the Third Engineer went to sleep and the water ran out. They burnt out one boiler and again our speed was reduced, we stopped for five hours and I had a talk with the Officer of the Watch. He said that another seven and a half minutes and the boiler would have burst. Many people would have been killed because of the way we are packed. The engineer in question is now travelling home as the plumber's assistant. That meant the second engineer had to be removed from his command on the ship and, since they were short-staffed to start the voyage, they have been obliged to call in Royal Navy and British Mercantile Marine personnel. Since they took over the engine room last night, the steam heating has come on again, the ventilators work and our speed has gone up from 11 to 15½ knots. This gives us a marvellous chance to get our own back on the Americans but what will happen if the story gets to the newspapers, I don't quite know.

Since we left Hawaii we've had about six different sets of orders but the skipper is set on going to San Francisco and nothing will sway him. We were ordered to Seattle but this was not a popular move, it means another three days in colder weather. There are many storms up there and for the past two days we have been riding on the edge of one. It has been pretty unpleasant with waves twenty feet high. The sea has always been on the port bow and a combined pitch and roll put many in their cabins. I have felt marvellous all the time and am looking forward to a good time in the States.

I must tell you an amusing story about Hawaii. You know the American ships are dry and we were very keen to get the where-withal for a party. We had been talking and playing bridge with a very nice American nurse who happened to be detailed for special duty with the Transport Commander who had had a heart attack. He went ashore in Hawaii in a litter and she went with him in the ambulance. He was detained and she came back on board with the litter. My great friend, Percy Hope-Johnstone, and I were stand-ing on deck when this litter was carried past the Military Police, she walked beside it with an innocent, demure look on her face. This was too much for us and we had to leave in case we gave the show away. We had a very good party.

Breakfast is early tomorrow so that we can all be on deck when we sail under the Golden Gate Bridge. We will disembark before lunch and go to a big hospital in San Francisco itself. I expect that a good number will be detained and hope that the rest of us go speedily across to an east coast port and then home. The two *Queens* are doing the Atlantic crossing running on a schedule so we will probably go home on one of them. Fortunately they are not so crowded going east so we should have a pleasant four days.

There is then a gap of seven days in my letter; this was the time we spent in San Francisco and it is no wonder that I did not have time to write. There can be few finer sights in the world than the view you get sailing under the Golden Gate Bridge. Cape Town harbour with Table Mountain in the background is impressive but it just lacks something.

We were sorry to say goodbye to the crew of the *Marine Shark* who had treated us so well. They had put on a special dinner with every course named after an event in our captivity; it was Filet Mignon Mountbatten and Poached Japanese Salmon with McArthur Sauce ending up with Cake à la Golden Gate.

When we landed in San Francisco we were taken to a large American Camp on Angel Island which is in San Francisco Bay and not very far from Alcatraz. We could see all the details of the security measures and the armed guards patrolling the perimeter. It looked a bleak forbidding place. Our camp was very different and once more we were in the hands of people who understood our problems and did their very best to help us. The first task was to equip us with uniforms that looked a little more like our own British Army dress. Canadian battle dress was warm and smart and many of us had managed to save some item of uniform from our original equipment. I had guarded jealously my Royal Artillery forage cap with its unusual shape and distinctive blue and red colours. We were also given some pay but that seemed very mean and we soon set out to see if we could add to that miserly sum.

A ferry ran regularly between Angel Island and the mainland and we soon found our way to San Francisco. The banks were very trusting and, provided you had proof of identity and could remember the address of your bank, they would advance $20. The problem was to convince more than one bank that you were a responsible citizen and a good financial risk.

We were required to report once in every twenty-four hours even though we did not have to sleep in the camp. My normal schedule was to report before breakfast, eat breakfast and then go back to San Francisco. Breakfast was a wonderful meal, we moved past a succulent lot of dishes eggs, bacon, muffins, etc., etc. I remember to this day being asked whether I wanted, 'Marmalade?' and when I said, 'Yes, please,' it was slapped all over my bacon. I suppose it is logical if you have apple sauce with pork but I have never got used to marmalade with my bacon.

I have never experienced such hospitality as we were accorded in San Francisco. A number of us had been together since the prison camp in Mukden and we were known – or called ourselves – 'The Ten Horsemen'. Why this was so I quite forget but all the others had been in yeomanry regiments, the majority in the Lanarkshire Yeomanry. Percy Hope-Johnstone and I had been friends since the awful days in Formosa and I had a great regard for his attitude as a prisoner of war. It must have been so much more difficult for men who had left wives and young families at home – it was bad enough for me as a bachelor. It was some time after the end of the war that his son, after a battle which lasted 193 years, was granted the title of 'Earl of Annandale and Hartfell' in Dumfriesshire. The ten of us decided that we would have one great celebration dinner.

It was decided that I, as usual, would be the treasurer and we started by going to 'The Top of the Mark' for drinks; the view from the bar at the top of the Mark Hopkins Hotel is so spectacular that you have to queue to get a table to have a drink – but it is well worth it in the end. I was not so enthusiastic as I suffer from vertigo after a climbing accident – but everyone else enjoyed it. From there we took ourselves to the St. Francis Hotel which had, and I'm sure still has, the reputation of being one of the best restaurants in that part of the world. The scheme was that everyone could eat what he fancied but I should try to keep track of the cost and, as each dish was ordered, I would call upon a contribution from the individual concerned. It amazed me to see how many of our party ordered dishes with rice and to this day I still like rice – but, as I finish the meal I have one spoonful with salt to remind me of the days when that was all I had.

I suppose we had been without money for so long that we were quite unused to the idea of spending it. Today I'm sure that if the ten of us went out to dinner together, we would agree to go 'Dutch' and split the bill. Not so then, every dish had a price on it, the money was paid into the pool and the cash in front of me grew and grew. After a wonderful evening the time came to settle the bill and I called our waiter for the reckoning. Imagine my surprise when he said, 'You don't owe anything, it has all been settled.' When I asked how this had come about he replied, 'That American General across the room has paid the bill.' I went to express my thanks and the thanks of the rest of the table and the General said, 'I'm delighted to be able to do this. I've spent a lot of the war in England and your people were very kind to me, this is an attempt to repay some of that kindness.' He then took us all back to his apartment for drinks with his wife and lovely daughter. My main problem was to remember who had paid what so that, having collected all the money, I could distribute it again.

San Francisco is a very colourful city and we certainly made the most of our time there. One evening we were entertained by The Ancient Order of Buffaloes and got out of their bar in the early hours of the morning, just in time to report for roll-call in our camp. Everyone was so generous and kind and we saw a lot of the city and the countryside surrounding it. I vowed that I would go back if at all possible and finally achieved my ambition when I was able to take my family twenty years later when I retired from my job in the Malayan Civil Service.

The time went all too quickly but we were glad to be on the next stage of our journey home. From San Francisco we were taken to a camp near Tacoma just south of Seattle – Fort Lewis was an American Army depot. Once again we were treated most royally, dances with nurses in the Officer's Mess and, of course, as much good food as one could eat. By this time the majority of us had made a pretty spectacular recovery, we had put on weight and ate and drank pretty well what we liked. From Fort Lewis we boarded a Canadian National train for our trip to New York across Canada. We travelled in great luxury in Pullman cars and the scenery was quite out of this world. Unless one has seen the grandeur of the Rockies it is difficult to describe the thrill of travelling through the valleys with the huge mountains towering above the railway. One constantly marvelled at the skill of the engineers who built the track.

By this time we had become accustomed to having a small 'snort' before lunch and before dinner but the problem was getting an adequate supply. On the way across Canada we developed a commando-type operation; at each stop a number of us would try to cash cheques at the nearest bank while others established themselves in the queue at the local liquor store. We ran into some unusual customs; in some provinces it was illegal to buy liquor standing up so you had to sit down at a table to order. We quickly learned the new tricks and had a very enjoyable trip.

Having given letter writing a miss once we got to San Francisco, I started again on the train.

> Near Vancouver.
> 7th November 1945

I continue my letter on a Canadian National Pullman car on my way to New York across Canada. This, as you see, is the eve of brother Hugh's twenty-first birthday, how I should like to be with him now.

The account of our time between landing in San Francisco and the present moment would take pages and until I see you and talk to you I can't tell you just how we have been treated. We went to a big American camp on 1st November and got our pay and uniforms. We have Canadian battle dress which is very warm and quite smart. Pay as usual is short but I managed to cash a cheque yesterday for $40. A dollar goes just about as far as a shilling, haircuts are $1 and one's money slips away very easily. I have managed to buy a few little things which I am bringing home.

The people in America have been wonderful to us. In San Francisco I never went to bed in my bunk at all. They took us to their houses, out to parties and on the last day two of us had a big convertible coupé at our disposal. Life is very normal here and it is a most wonderful country; I would not have missed the trip for anything.

From San Francisco we moved to Fort Lewis just south of Seattle. Tacoma is the town near the fort and once again we were entertained regally. Last night we took some nurses out to dinner and then danced at the Officers' Club. Everyone is so friendly and one feels at home immediately. Lots of American officers have been stationed in England and we are weighted down with addresses of people whom we must contact in various parts of the country to tell them that these officers are home and happy. Many want to go back to England and I have an idea that the picture of awful conditions which we have formed from newspaper accounts is very exaggerated.

We sail from New York on the *Queen Mary* on 12th November and will be in England on the 17th. I hope there will be some mail in New York. Sir George Sansom is still in our Embassy in Washington so I wrote to Lady Sansom and boldly told her that I was coming. I hope to see them and, if they asked me to stay, it would be wonderful. We will have no time in New York as it is. If we had been there when we should have, on the 4th, we were to have eight days as guests of the American Red Cross and other organisations.

I'm afraid that most of us are returning home with a nasty taste in our mouths. The British Government has done absolutely nothing to help us and we owe everything to the Americans. The few times when our staff officers have to arrange anything they always make a mess of things. Today we had to walk nearly two miles with our luggage because someone had forgotten to order the transport. It is a funny thing but the Army has a happy way of choosing the most unsuitable people for liaison work over here.

9th November 1945

I am going to finish this now and have it sent by the Red Cross man on the train. It is a bit difficult to write as we are doing about sixty miles an hour across the plains of Canada. The snow is lying on the fields and the sun is already high in a beautiful clear blue sky. It is a fine country and we are enjoying our trip very much. The food is marvellous, I've just finished a breakfast of tomato juice, porridge, bacon and four eggs, toast and coffee. There are ten of us on the train known as the 'Ten Horsemen' and we had a party last night to celebrate brother Hugh's birthday. I wish he could have been with us, I'm sure he would be very popular.

We expect to be in England on the 17th or the morning of the 18th, I believe a civic reception has been arranged at Southampton. The *Queen Mary* is making her last trip as a troopship and they are going to celebrate her marvellous work during the war.

I am looking forward so much to being home that I can scarcely allow myself to think. I do hope I can see you both very soon. It's a long time ago but I can picture you as though it were yesterday. My love to you both.

Without any doubt at all, the high spot of our journey home was the trip across Canada by Canadian National Railways. We went through places like Banff, Jasper National Park and Saskatoon in Saskatchewan. The scenery was quite magnificent and we took turns to share the observation floor on the top of one of the coaches. The Rockies towered above the track as the train wound its way round the tight corners that followed the fast-flowing rivers. Many of the bends were so tight that you could see half the front part of the train from a position in the back carriages.

The magnificence of the Rockies was followed by the endless wheatlands of Canada, flat as far as the eye could see. It is difficult to realise just what a vast country Canada is; day after day the train took us across that great country until we arrived at Albany in the State of New York. It says something for our powers of recovery, and the excellent treatment that we had had at the hands of the Americans, that we were able to enjoy the trip, the food and the service to the full. And to think that all that luxury was paid for by His Majesty's Government – but I reckon we deserved it, and more.

Chapter 15

The Last Lap

I had managed to get the group for which I was responsible across Canada without too many 'fall outs' and was looking forward to handing the whole thing over to someone else and seeing something of New York. But, it was not to be. For some reason there had developed a very unusual attitude to the released P.O.W.s amongst the staff officers sent to organise our trip across the Atlantic. They seemed to think that we were all on the verge of a nervous breakdown and not to be trusted with any unsupervised freedom. They imagined that we had forgotten the meaning of military discipline and that we would throw over the traces at the first opportunity. This attitude resulted in our not being allowed ashore in New York; we were driven straight from the train to the *Queen Mary* and looked longingly at that bustling city from its decks.

She had been used as a troopship throughout the war and had carried thousands of British and American soldiers. Part of the time we were told the ship had operated the 'hot bunk' system whereby two men shared a bunk; while one was sleeping the other was feeding and exercising. We were more fortunate and four of us shared one of the staterooms which cost a king's ransom in peacetime. The regular steward looked after us and we could not have been in better hands. He was a mine of information about the ship and had a wonderful memory about the things that had happened while we had been out of circulation.

I knew that my mother had joined my father in Nigeria and, at one point, I had hoped that it would be possible for me to join them direct from America. But that was too difficult to manoeuvre for the British Army and I went straight home. I felt sure that my mother would come home and that my father would join us as soon as he could get leave. He was the Chief Commissioner of the Northern Provinces, had been knighted some years previously and was very much involved in the plans for constitutional change in Nigeria. It seemed that I might not see him for some time so I wrote at some length about my hopes for the future and news of my immediate past.

On Board *Queen Mary*
15th November 1945

My dear Dad,

I address this letter to you alone because I hope that when I arrive home I will find Mother there or else on her way home. I do wish you could come home, somehow I must see you after so much has happened to our family. Writing is such a poor substitute for sitting down with you and having a real talk. I don't think you would see much change in me, I admit I have a moustache of which I am extremely proud. It has taken me the best part of my captivity to get it to its present state of magnificence. Mentally I feel fine and am still as lighthearted and gay as I used to be. I think the poor people like yourself worried much more than we did. We were so intent on keeping out of trouble that we did not have much time to worry.

I have heard it said, 'It's so easy to remember but so hard to forget.' I have found the exact opposite, we are still being asked to fill out reports and 'atrocity forms', and really they have little meaning now. We are so glad to be free and so anxious to put our contact with the Japanese behind us that this perpetual questioning becomes rather annoying. I have now filled in about six separate interrogation forms and today was presented with my seventh.

These last two days have been most pleasant as I met a Mr. and Mrs. Mckay who are returning from Canada, where he spent his leave from Nigeria. He was in Ibadan and is in the process of transferring to the Geological Survey Dept. He saw you quite recently and I have put him through a long questioning. He admires you very much and has said some very fine things about you. It made me feel very proud of you. Unfortunately he has never met Mother so could tell me nothing about her. He said you were the most accessible Resident in Nigeria but that in your present position you were surrounded with such a galaxy of underlings that your accessibility had suffered slightly. He gave me an impression of Kaduna that I had never had before. I'm not sure whether he exaggerated but it sounds like a Court comparable with St. James's, with yourself on the throne. I should love to come out to see you in your exalted position.

When I arrived in New York I got some letters from Aunt Doris and Hepscott. Aunt Sarah said she had some for me from you and I am looking forward so much to reading them. I'm sorry more of us could not be present at cousin Miriam's wedding. Uncle informs me with pride that he expects to be a grandfather in the middle of next year. No time wasted. I'm sorry that Mac had to go abroad so soon after the wedding. I don't know whether he intends to stay in the Army. It is certainly not the life for me and I doubt if Miriam would like it, but of course I do not know her now. Everybody must have changed so much in the four and a half years I have been away.

I'm afraid that the difference in the treatment we have had from our own people since we came on board this ship, and the marvellous hospitality we received from the Americans, has made us very bitter. We have a set of staff officers on board who are self-satisfied incompetent prigs. We have had many battles with them and some very harsh words have been spoken. We were on this ship thirty-six hours in New York and no-one was allowed ashore and no-one could come to see us. Sir George Sansom sent me a telegram and asked me to ring him up but permission to do this was refused. Unfortunately we found out too late that some regulation had been published under which we are considered to be 'mental patients' until we have completed forty-two days leave. As such we cannot be disciplined under the Army Act. Never have I heard of anything quite so stupid. None of the men are as good as they used to be but they cannot be classed as mental cases. Nobody will give them an order, the cabins in which they live are filthy and the men are getting slowly out of hand. If we had been allowed to handle them as we have done for the last three and a half years there would have been no trouble. Instead of detailing men for mess orderlies on a roster, they asked for volunteers; this resulted in eighty per cent missing dinner the first night and fifty per cent missing lunch the next day. If the papers get hold of the story, I'm afraid questions will be asked.

I had a most wonderful time in America and would very much like to go back there. We came across the Pacific with seventy-nine American Army nurses and had a most enjoyable trip. I fell for one quite badly but as usual that is all over now. She was much older than I am and we have an example of the unfortunate situation that can cause in our own family. Another girl, the wife of a Major in the 1st Cavalry Regiment, saw all this happening and told me not to be so stupid. She knew the other girl very well, said we could never be happy and that she would ruin me in three years. I'm glad I took her advice and she became a great friend. When we left the ship she gave me an air force chronometer made by Hamilton as a parting present. She had worn it herself but it is too big for a lady's watch and now looks fine on my wrist. I lost the watch you and Mother gave me in 1939 about two years ago. Just where it went I do not know but I think it was stolen. They had a tremendous value in prison camp and could be traded for a lot of extra food with the Japanese guards.

This really is an amazing ship. One can travel for days without ever seeing the sea. Of course, most of her lounges and swimming pools have been converted to bunks or mess halls but the officers still have the use of a large lounge which seats about 500 at a cinema show. There are four of us in a stateroom on the main deck which usually has two occupants. There is a private bathroom and we are very comfortable. Our steward, a man called Gates, has looked after Churchill and many other celebrities. Ten of us have formed ourselves into a small club called 'The Ten Horsemen' and Gates said that, in his thirty years at sea, he has never met a more amusing set of people. This is a great compliment as he must have met a lot of amusing people in that time. The ten of us have travelled together on the ship from Manila and right across the States. We have had a very good time and are all great friends. We are trying to plan a reunion in London, seven of us are Gunners and the other three are Squadron Leaders in the R.A.F. One is a doctor and another a most amusing man who hails from Cork and therefore maintains that he is neutral. He holds the George Cross for a magnificent show on a bombed aerodrome before he left England.

I wish you were here to discuss the next part of my letter with me. I have not changed in my intention to try and become a Colonial Administrative Officer half as good as yourself. I liked Malaya and would like to go back there to help put the country in order. I have talked to Mr. Mckay and he says the best man to see is the Colonial Office Liaison Officer at the Crown Agents. He will be able to put me in touch with the man I should see in the Colonial Office. I intend to do this at the earliest opportunity so I can arrange my leave. I think they will want me back pretty quickly because so many of our officers were lost and there is so much to do in the country. I gather there is a new scheme for leave but Mckay did not know whether or not it applied to Malaya . . . If it does it might be worth my while to put some leave on ice and take a longer leave in two years time when conditions are more normal in England. I don't think I am going to like England in its present state, everything that I like seems to be unobtainable or very expensive. I see no prospect of being able to run a car and life without one for me is not very enjoyable. Clothes seem to be very difficult, I have absolutely nothing left of the beautiful wardrobe I took out to Malaya and you know how I like good clothes. I hope to be able to get a good allowance of coupons and intend to apply to as many people as possible.

I gather the Colonial Office has treated its officers who went into the services very well and I hope I shall find that my salary has been raised. If I go back as an Assistant District Officer, Mckay says I should be on £650-700 a year. I will keep in close touch with you on this subject and would be most grateful if you could tell me someone I could see in London who could advise me. It is so difficult when one has been out of things for so long. If Mother is at home I know she will be able to help me almost as much as yourself.

I wonder what my brother Hugh is going to do; does he intend to follow in the footsteps already made by you or is he intending to branch out on his own? I gather that the Irawaddy Bridgehead Battle in which his regiment played a distinguished part is reckoned to be one of the toughest scraps in this war.

18th October 1945

I finish this now because we dock tomorrow and I have my kit to sort out and pack. I am going to Liverpool and then to Hepscott. I hope to be there on Monday or Tuesday, today being Saturday. I gather they are pretty good with us and we will have forty-two days leave before discharge.

Next letter will tell you all about my arrival home and at last I will have some letters from you to answer.
                                Your loving son.

We docked in Liverpool and not Southampton so the great spectacular welcome for the *Queen Mary* did not happen. We were warned to keep our baggage under constant guard as some P.O.W.s who had returned before us had found their kit-bags rifled and all valuables stolen. As we had bought and had been given hundreds of American cigarettes and numerous pairs of nylons, they were an attractive haul. But, how mean can a man get to steal from returning prisoners?

We were processed with reasonable speed in Liverpool and soon I was on my way to my second home at Hepscott. I can still remember, forty-five years later, the warm feeling when I saw the robust figure of my uncle Munro Simpson, standing just as he said he would, under the big clock in the middle of the Central Station in Newcastle-on-Tyne. He only had a very limited amount of petrol but he had saved enough for me to travel home in style. What a welcome I got from my Aunt and my cousins and we talked until well into the night. How wonderful it was to sleep again in my own bed.

Chapter 16

Time to Reflect

I have often been asked, 'What were your feelings about the Japanese, once you were released?' The answer is that I do not know. All I wanted to do was to put the three and a half years of captivity behind me, forget all about it and, as soon as possible, get down to work and a normal life again. The fact that I wanted to forget all about my time with the Japanese is the reason for this chapter being written in September 1991 rather than 1951.

We have just heard of the release of John McCarthy and Jackie Mann. Little has, so far, been said about the conditions in which they were confined – in deference, no doubt, to Terry Waite and the other hostages still held, but it is clear that they suffered brutality and deprivation that made some aspects of our captivity a veritable health farm. It says a tremendous amount for their courage and moral strength that both were able to endure long periods of torture and solitary confinement. How could one human being inflict such suffering on another – and to what end?

That I think is the main feeling that I had about the Japanese. But, I certainly came to the conclusion that they had a deep inferiority complex about the white races and, in particular, any member of those races who looked down on them physically. Tall members of our prisoners were likely to get a much more drastic beating than the shorter variety.

We were seldom supervised by Japanese personnel. The local conscripts in Formosa, Japan and Manchuria were responsible, under a Japanese officer, for guarding us and organising the work fatigues. The Japanese were as hard on them as they were on us. Physical beatings were frequent and a blitz on the guards was poor news for us.

The way the Japanese organised supplies from the Red Cross was always a cause for great concern. They seemed to take a great delight in playing a 'cat and mouse game', showing us huge truck loads of supplies at a railway siding and then saying that orders had to come from Tokyo before they could be released. We then went through the pantomime of having to open every tin in case it contained parts for a machine gun! Throughout our captivity we had difficulty in deciding whether the Japanese who administered the Prisoner of War Camps were stupid, sadistic or just filled with low cunning and hatred. We were often moved to think how it was that one human being could be so unaffected by the suffering of others. Having read much about the history of the war, I have come to the conclusion that the Japanese had, and probably still have, a totally different attitude to life. They were astounded that so many prisoners had surrendered and had not committed suicide – or hari-kiri. It was very clear in Singapore that they were quite unprepared for the number of prisoners who surrendered. For weeks we were looking after ourselves with very little help from the Japanese. Throughout our captivity we were taunted with the statement that we should have been glorious dead rather than prisoners.

Even though I had tried to put the tribulations of the last three years out of my mind, I could not but think back to the war in Malaya, ending with the surrender of Singapore, and to wonder if anything could have been done differently. I must stress that the views that follow are my own personal views and opinions.

I had been commissioned in England and had seen the effect of the bombing by the German air force and the mobilisation of the country to fight what then appeared to be a war we were unlikely to win. Even the Americans were slightly sceptical about our ability to win through. But there was a spirit of great determination and a tremendous confidence amongst the ordinary people in the street. They accepted the sacrifices and hard times with good humour and a willingness to help each other. Malaya seemed to be very unprepared and the hope was that it 'would never happen here'. The war in Europe seemed a long way off and the defensive preparations for the general public almost non-existent. I have already written about the Volunteers, men who were excellent linguists and who knew the country well had been formed into infantry units and called up from their important jobs at the outset of hostilities. I am sure this was a mistake, they would have been much better employed as liaison officers to the British and Australian forces. Through no fault of their own, these troops could not tell the difference between a Chinese, a Japanese or a Malay – and they had no means of finding out. Many of the volunteers were taken prisoner as privates or non-commissioned officers and had a very hard time as prisoners of war.

When I got to Singapore, having escaped from Trengganu, I was amazed to see how normal life was. I suppose there was a certain amount of bravado and 'stiff upper lip' about people's behaviour but there seemed to be hundreds of wives and children who should have been shipped out of the country at a much earlier stage. The scenes on the docks when they finally tried to leave were dreadful and many perished during the bombing raids or drowned when their ships were sunk near Singapore. The view from England seemed to be that Singapore was a garrison – a sort of fort or armed camp. It was not, it was a thriving commercial city with very little in the way of fortifications apart from the army headquarters in Fort Canning. This had its battle headquarters and very substantial defences.

Why were the defences throughout Malaya and Singapore not stronger? I think one must go back to the position of the British in that country. We were there as a protecting power and we could not make Singapore an impregnable fortress and leave the rest of Malaya to the mercy of an invader. I suppose it might have been possible to construct a strong defensive position across the middle of the country – the Muar-Mersing line. But how would you explain to the Rulers, and their peoples north of that line, that they were to be left to defend themselves? Similarly there was the problem high-lighted so often in the Press, about the 'Guns that faced the wrong way'. I have already written something about this problem. The guns were fortress artillery, designed and positioned to repel an attack on Singapore from the sea.

These huge guns fired shells weighing about half a ton, they were ponderous to load and fire and quite ineffective against troops in the jungle. Had they been facing towards the land and not the sea, they would have been firing over the palaces of the Sultan of Johore. He was one of the greatest supporters of the British cause and, if my memory is accurate, had contributed from his own personal fortune enough money to purchase three Spitfire fighters for the R.A.F. Huge armour-piercing shells were not the answer when the Japanese forces were commandeering bicycles from the local populace, using jungle tracks and outflanking our men at every step. I was told that, on one occasion, the Lancashire Yeomanry had withdrawn their 25-pounder guns no less than twenty miles, only to find themselves surrounded by Japanese troops within hours. It was a form of warfare for which our troops had had very little preparation.

Towards the end of hostilities on 29th January, the main body of the British 18th Division arrived. Within three weeks they were all to become prisoners of war. Many people had said that it was a mistake to land the troops and, even at that late stage, they should have been diverted and lived to fight another day. In his book, General Percival does not support that view and holds that when the decision was taken to send the Division to Singapore it was the intention to hold the island for as long as possible. That they should make so small a contribution and become prisoners so soon was 'just the luck of war'.

The Division was commanded by Maj. Gen. M. Beckwith-Smith, a man who inspired all who met him. His death from diphtheria in Formosa prison camp was a great shock to us all. He was a small, neat person who had chosen as his A.D.C. a very tall Welsh Guardsman, Archie Bevan, who became a firm friend of mine throughout our captivity.

It is not for me to comment on the organisation of Higher Command but, as a young officer, I did find it very confusing. Sir Shenton Thomas was Governor and Commander-in-Chief, General Percival was General Officer Commanding Malaya and Mr. Duff Cooper had come to Singapore as 'Cabinet representative in the Far East'. General Sir Archibald Wavell was Commander-in-Chief and there were other very imposing figures like Sir George Sansom to head the Ministry of Information Far East. The Navy and the Air Force had their own chiefs and responsible to General Percival were Lt. Gen. Sir Lewis Heath commanding 3rd Indian Corps, Maj. Gen. Gordon Bennett commanding the A.I.F. and Maj. Gen. Keith Simmons commanding the Singapore Fortress. It was an impressive list but in reality the troops under their command were inexperienced in modern warfare.

Could anything have been done differently? I rather doubt it. Talking to General Percival while we were in Changi prison camp, I was so impressed with the global view he was able to take, even though he had suffered so much. The struggle in Europe meant that supplies which might have saved Singapore had to be sent to Russia and the Middle East. He accepted that this was the right decision. I believe he was a big man in all respects.

Chapter 17

How Did We Survive?

The title of this chapter is 'How did we survive?' I wish I knew but there are some thoughts – even so long ago. It is difficult for any committed Christian to come to terms with the suffering which war brings. One is tempted to say 'If there is a God, why should all this happen?' I saw so much individual suffering that my faith was put to the test. 'Why,' I asked myself, '*did* all this have to happen?' I don't think there was any answer and many of us continued to worship when the opportunity was allowed. The Japanese had an ambivalent attitude to our Christian services; on the one hand they regarded them as potentially subversive but, against that, they did not wish to be accused of suppressing all forms of worship. When we were not forced to go out to work on Sundays, we took the opportunity to celebrate Holy Communion. Throughout my captivity Padré Stallard did his best to ensure that we were able to take bread and wine. The bread was often compressed rice grains and the wine a sticky fruit syrup supplied in our general ration, but the services were not interrupted by the Japanese. We were forbidden to sing the National Anthem but 'Onward Christian Soldiers' and 'Jerusalem' were rendered with great gusto.

In contrast to the hostages in Lebanon, we had our friends with us all the time. Very few people were kept in solitary confinement and I just cannot imagine how awful it must have been to be deprived of daylight and fresh air for such a long period. We were able to discuss matters in normal terms, the only thing we had to watch was the odd 'fifth columnist' who was likely to give the Japanese sufficient information to suspect that we had a clandestine source of information.

The worst aspect of our captivity was not knowing what would happen on the morrow. We were always surrounded by rumour: 'People were about to move to another camp', 'Red Cross parcels would be distributed within a matter of days', 'A visit from the Swiss Protecting Power would take place soon'. It was all very disturbing but we soon learned to live with this atmosphere.

How can one comment on the 'will to survive'? I spent a lot of my captivity working in camp hospitals and I have a lot of regard for the work done by our doctors. They had very few drugs or medicines and had to make the difficult decision to give the drugs to those patients who were most likely to survive. I saw men who did not appear to be desperately ill turn their faces to the wall and die; I saw others, who appeared to be at death's door, rally and survive to the end.

Above all else, I believe that it was the friendships that developed that enabled us to survive. There was a bond which cemented us against the Japanese, the common enemy. When one of our friends was ill, we would collect rations and Red Cross supplies to hasten his recovery. Above all else, one had to retain a sense of humour and proportion, difficult though that proved to be on many occasions.

As each birthday or Christmas came and went, there was always the hope that it would be our last as prisoners. A card, signed by the other thirty-five members of my squad, read 'A SIGNAL MESSAGE Xmas 1943. Best Wishes for Christmas. May 1944 bring something better than Water.' But it was not to be and we still had another Christmas to spend in captivity.

Reading the signatures today brings back many memories of the friends who stood together in those dark days.

Brian Humphreys, Lt. Gen. Sir Lewis Heath's A.D.C., who had been British American Tobacco's man in India before he was called up to the reserves. He had a fund of stories and always managed to put the best possible light on our tribulations. He had a wonderful command of the English language and his description of our hosts cannot be printed.

Percy Hope-Johnstone, a Major in the Lanarkshire Yeomanry who was an inspiration to us all. He never wavered in his dislike of the Japanese. In 1985 Percy's son became the Earl of Annandale and Hartfell, reviving a family title which had been in abeyance for 193 years. It must have been particularly upsetting for married men with young families, waiting for news of them at home. It was bad enough for me as a bachelor.

Tom Mangnall, a tall dark Lancastrian always thinking about his return to those wonderful golf courses near Formby, which was his home club.

Archie Bevan, Maj. Gen. Beckwith-Smith's A.D.C.; at some point in his life he had been connected with the stage and organised what little entertainment we were allowed.

Jim Wright, an Engineer, and my bridge opponent for many years. I played with 'Tab' Tabeart and I do believe that being allowed to play the odd game certainly kept us sane. The Japanese actually provided us with packs of playing cards.

Frank Grazebook, a tall man, Major in the Royal Engineers. His very height annoyed the Japanese and he would always be selected for any beatings that might be the order of the day.

Sidney Downer one of the few Australians in our camp. He was a Squadron Leader in the R.A.A.F. and had to take a good amount of ribbing – which he did with great good humour.

Things were always pretty grim but it was our ability to band together against the Japanese and look for the light at the end of the tunnel – it was a long time in coming. Conditions in Formosa and Japan were very grim but they improved when we went to Manchuria. I suppose we were lucky not to be there during the winter even though we did have proper brick-built barracks and not the coolie lines in which we were housed in the camps in Formosa. Our treatment became less brutal and the officers were not forced to work but a number did. It was not unpleasant doing the odd spot of gardening and I went back to help in the camp hospital. By that time the Japanese must have accepted that they were not going to win the war and their attitude to us changed considerably. There were no more beatings, food was better and there was no forced labour for the officers. When we got to Mukden, I think all of us felt that, barring accidents or illness, we had a good chance of survival.

I do not think that any of us realised just how close to death we might have been. It was years later, when reading the history of the last days of the war, that I had an inkling of how close an escape we had. If the Emperor had not over-ruled his Chiefs of the Army and Navy, there would have been one gigantic battle culminating, I have little doubt, in the invasion of Japan. There would have been hundreds of thousands of casualties on both sides; the Japanese civilian population would have fought to the last with bamboo spears and other home-made weapons. As it was, the die-hard Army senior officers made an attempt to capture the recording made by the Emperor saying that Japan must surrender. Far-sightedly, the Emperor's personal staff suspected that such an attempt would be made and they arranged for a copy of the recording to be made and sent to the Broadcasting Station by a different route.

If an invasion of Japan had taken place, there is little doubt that all prisoners of war would have been killed. Cyril Wild was the interpreter for General Percival at the surrender of Singapore. Subsequently he worked on the Siam Railway and witnessed the appalling atrocities perpetrated by the Japanese when they built it. He gave evidence at the War Crimes Tribunals which resulted in so many Japanese being executed and others being sentenced to long terms of imprisonment. Not all the war criminals were prosecuted as a substantial number had committed suicide once they appreciated the enormity of their deeds – and the fact that Japan had lost the war. Cyril Wild worked for a year after the Japanese surrender to bring the criminals to justice and, just as he saw the possible end of his labours and could look forward to a well-earned holiday with his family, he was killed in an air crash in Hong Kong in September 1946. James Bradley has written a wonderful appreciation of Wild's work entitled *Cyril Wild. The Tall Man Who Never Slept*, published by Woodfield Publishing in 1991.

As I have indicated earlier in this book, the Japanese were absolutely obsessed with the idea of anyone escaping. This, at the outset of our captivity, caused many unpleasant and even violent incidents as the Japanese insisted on prisoners signing a quite illegal 'non-escape clause'. A document produced at the trial of General Tojo and addressed to the Commanding General Taiwan P.O.W. Camps set out what action should be taken in the event of the likelihood of prisoners escaping.

The Methods: (a) Whether they are destroyed individually or in groups, or however it is done, with mass bombing, poisonous smoke, poisons, drowning, decapitation, or what, dispose of them as the situation dictates. (b) In any case it is the aim not to allow the escape of a single one, to annihilate them all, and not to leave any traces.

I have no doubt that similar orders were in force in Mukden.

To George
FROM Jock

Best wishes for
Christmas —
May 1944 bring something
better than Water!

XMAS.
1943

A
SIGNAL
MESSAGE

THIS YEAR NEXT YEAR?

Members of my squad who signed a Christmas card in Shirawaka Camp 1943. I have been unable to decipher one or two signatures and some of the initials may not be correct.

T. B. Magnall	G. A. J (Archie) Bevan
J. L. Badgett	P. W. (Percy) Hope Johnstone
M. Anderson	G. Moss
R. Kennedy	J. Mackenzie
J (Jim) Wright	O. N. (Ossie) Diamond
G. Murray Stewart	R. Delme Radcliffe
J. Brown	Sydney F. Downer
O. R. Sewell	G. H. Forbes
G. Fifield	M. W. Chapman
D. (Tabs) Tabeart	Geoffrey Fennell
B (Brian) Humphrey	Frank Grazebrook
J. Cross Pedley	R. Dinwiddie
J. W. Bindeman	J. Fairbairn
E. S. Priest	

Chapter 18

Rehabilitation

Even though I had suffered from some of the most unpleasant and debilitating diseases, I was still only twenty-five years of age when I was released. I was soon putting on weight and very anxious to get back to Malaya.

Much of my time on leave was spent catching up with old friends. Of four of my very old friends, three had been at school, medical students at Newcastle Royal Victoria Infirmary, and by the time I got home they were qualified medical practitioners. Christo Strang and Basil Holroyd were in the Navy, Raymond Dobson in the Army and Tommy Studdert in the R.A.F. It was through them that I met the girl who was to become my wife. Tommy Studdert got himself married in Somerset and the rest of us arranged to meet in London before going to the wedding. The others had set up a lunch at the Grosvenor House Hotel with two girls, Anne Worthington and Sheila Mohun. After the wedding I managed to see quite a lot of Anne before the time came for me to go back to Malaya.

We had received all sorts of encouraging missives from the King and the Secretary of State for the Colonies but those of us who were fit were very anxious to get back to work. The country, after the Japanese had surrendered, was placed under a British Military Administration staffed by those officers who had not been captured and others selected from the Services. There was an understandable feeling that the longer we were away from Malaya, the more likely our promotion prospects would be harmed. So we got another note from the Secretary of State saying 'not to worry'. (See Appendix.)

My mother came back from Nigeria soon after I arrived home, followed by my father when he could arrange his leave. We were all together in Penrith, where they had moved at the beginning of the war as my old school had moved across from the danger area of Newcastle. They had bought a house in the little village of Eamont Bridge on the road to Ullswater. It was a delightful place but I had few friends in the area, spent a lot of time going across to see my pals in Newcastle and generally making a nuisance of myself.

My father had expressed the view that the sooner I got back to Malaya, the better it would be for all concerned. Whether it was coincidence or not, but three days after he went to a meeting in the Colonial Office I got a letter telling me to report there.

On arrival I was told that I had been chosen to be Private Secretary to Malcolm MacDonald who was soon to take up his appointment as the first Governor-General. It would be my job to organise his private office so I was to spend some time getting to grips with codes and cyphers in the specialist department of the Colonial Office. Talk about being thrown in at the deep end!!

Chapter 19

Return to Malaya

After a brief spell in the Colonial Office in London, I got my sailing orders to go back to Malaya. My leave had been most enjoyable but, like all of my fellow Malayan Civil Service officers, we were anxious to get back to work. Many of us wondered just how we would be received by our old friends in the country, after all we had been responsible for their defence – and had not done all that great a job. It was quite heart-warming to see the welcome we got and the understanding that was shown to us. Never did I hear any criticism of the performance of the British services, there were no recriminations – just sympathy for the terrible times we had had as prisoners of war. After all, the Chinese in Singapore had suffered horribly at the hands of the Japanese.

There was, however, unspoken criticism of the performance of the civil service from the powers that be in the U.K. Such criticism was difficult to take from people who had not suffered in captivity; there was, for a number of years to come, a measure of hostility between those who had been captured and those who had for one reason or another 'got away'. Some had been on leave, others had been ordered to leave Singapore in the last few days of the battle. It took some years for this hostility to be forgotten. There were amongst the local population problems between those who had suffered torture at the hands of the Japanese and those who had collaborated with the occupying forces.

The trip out to Malaya was quite an experience. Old hands in the industry say that travel by air just after the war was really the height of commercial aviation – and I don't dispute that statement. We boarded a Sunderland Flying Boat of, I suppose, British Overseas Airways in Poole harbour. Our first stop, for lunch and re-fuelling, was Marseilles. Then on to Alexandria for our first night stop. A launch took us ashore and we were accommodated in excellent hotels all the way out to the Far East. One of the most interesting stop-overs, although we did not have much time to see the countryside, was at Habbaninyah, a huge lake in the middle of the desert just west of Baghdad. How the world has changed, I can't see British Airways flying there today!

I had a seat towards the back of the plane in the raised tail and had a wonderful view as we took off and came in to land. It was much more spectacular landing on the water than the slow measured descent of the present Jumbo Jets. As the planes were not pressurised they had a limited height ceiling and this sometimes resulted in an uncomfortable spell in rough weather. I remember looking along the fuselage and noting how much it flexed in bad weather.

We stopped at Karachi before the long flight over India to Calcutta. It was an unusual feeling to fly such a vast distance in a flying boat over a land mass in which there must have been few places where an emergency landing could be made. I have since flown many times between the U.K., the Far East, America and Australia and I can say that no trip was more enjoyable than the first one after the war. It lasted five days and we put down in that lovely island of Penang before finally landing in Singapore.

I had only a very short time to get myself organised before the arrival of His Excellency, the new Governor-General. The first problem which faced everyone was, where was he to live? Before the war Singapore and Malaya had been 'Godly and quietly governed' by one head, the Governor of Singapore and High Commissioner of Malaya, Sir Shenton Thomas, who resided at Government House in Singapore. After the war he was replaced by a Governor of Singapore. Sir Franklin Gimson, a Governor of the Malayan Union, Sir Edward Gent and a Governor-General Malcolm MacDonald. Also in the pack of cards was Lord Killearn, the Commissioner-General whose main responsibility was the distribution of food supplies, particularly rice, in Southeast Asia. Within measurable time would be added Governors of Sarawak and North Borneo and there was already a Resident in the Sultanate of Brunei.

Sir Edward Gent did not want the new Governor-General living in his territory, Sir Franklin Gimson was not keen to see him reside in Singapore, so a sort of compromise was struck for him to live in Penang. This was a Crown Colony, soon to become part of the Federation of Malaya, and the Resident S. N. (Fatty) King gave up his imposing Residency so that Malcolm MacDonald could have a house in keeping with his status. I know that M.M. was extremely grateful for this sacrifice as it solved a very knotty problem.

It might have solved one problem but it created many others and added up to an administrative nightmare for me. The general division of duties between the personal staff of a Governor is that the Private Secretary is responsible for all the office work, papers, communications with the U.K. Government and all official appointments, and the A.D.C. looks after the social side and any ceremonial occasions. The Governor-General had quite a large secretariat headed up by the Deputy Governor-General Maj. Gen. Sir Ralph Hone; unfortunately this was based in Singapore. Over the next few months we spent hours in R.A.F. planes flying between Penang, Singapore and sometimes Kuala Lumpur. Most correspondence had to be duplicated with the risk of sensitive material going astray and the delays caused in the post. The telephones had, generally, been restored after the ravages of the war but we had no scrambling devices and they had to be used circumspectly. Any top-secret despatches from London were sent by code and I spent many hours deciphering these long personal messages.

It soon became apparent that to have the Governor-General in Penang and his Deputy and secretariat 500 miles away in Singapore was very costly and adminstratively unsound. The search was mounted for a suitable residence in Singapore and the Sultan of Johore agreed that the Governor-General should use his Singapore Istana (palace). This was a gesture which was typical of that wonderful, larger than life character. Later in my Malayan Civil Service career I was posted to Johore as an Administrative Officer and saw what a great influence the Sultan had on the government of his State. He was always a stalwart supporter of the British cause before, during and after the War.

Tyersall was a small residence in comparison with the grandeur of Government House, a huge building on a hill in the middle of Singapore overlooking the whole of the City, where the Governor Sir Franklin Gimson lived. There was no room for Malcolm MacDonald's personal staff and his senior A.D.C. and I shared a small house not far away. Our main secretariat was in the Cathay Building in Singapore and this involved a lot of going and coming with papers, etc., etc., but it was a great improvement on the Penang set-up. We had very adequate secretarial and cipher staff and I was spared the long hours glued to code books.

Chapter 20

Life with Malcolm MacDonald

The purpose of this book was to record for my family my early life in Malaya and my experiences as a Prisoner of War with the Japanese. This I feel I have done, but a fitting end would be for me to set down some of the high-lights of the two years when I worked on Malcolm MacDonald's staff as his private secretary.

It is not my intention to write a biography of Malcolm MacDonald, nor am I qualified to do so, but I have often been asked to say how I enjoyed my time with him and what sort of a man he was. I can say, without doubt, that the two years I spent on his staff were the most interesting and the most influential period of my Colonial Service career. I was lucky to be at the centre of tremendous changes in the Government of Malaya.

M.M. was, to me, two different people. Outwardly he was a most charming individual and a supreme politician. He had a fantastic memory both in the short-term and for events long ago. I remember on one occasion he dictated a speech first thing in the morning and gave it five hours later, when he opened a new bank, without altering a word or a punctuation mark. He insisted that the text could be given to the press for the afternoon editions and that it would be as he had dictated it.

As a boss he was a hard task-master and one of the problems with him was that he had never been a 'small man'. He believed that everything was possible provided he said it should happen. On one occasion we were due to fly from Singapore to Kuala Lumpur in the late afternoon in an R.A.F. aircraft and the weather closed in and made flying impossible. M.M.'s reaction was, 'But they must fly as I have an important meeting tomorrow morning.' I said that I had already pointed out the importance of the meeting but the decision rested with the pilot of the plane and I was certain that the Air Officer Commanding would support his pilot. In the

Taken in Malaya when the author was Private Secretary to Malcolm MacDonald.

event we drove to K.L. in the Rolls in atrocious weather, I shared the driving with our Chinese chauffeur, and His Excellency slept most of the way. Our motor-cycle police escort managed less than twenty miles.

Great changes were taking place throughout the Commonwealth and Indian Independence was already in sight. M.M. had a vision of self-government for Malaya and Singapore and a brief to further this process. It was interesting to see how the local politicians in Malaya were very anxious to accelerate this process. The Chinese in Singapore were not particularly enthusiastic about taking part in local or national politics. Provided there was a stable political climate in which they could expand their commercial interests, they were more than happy.

M.M. had to face the criticisms of the Malays concerning the attempt to foist on the country, without consultation and without real concern for the position of the Rulers, a new constitution cooked up in Whitehall. The Rulers were reduced to mere religious figureheads and their state governments to provincial administrations. When the British Military Administration handed over to Sir Edward Gent, the new Governor of the Malayan Union, in April 1946, every Malayan Ruler and politician boycotted his installation. By this action the British had united the Malays in a new nationalism under their leader, Onn bin Ja'afar, who founded the United Malays National Organisation. M.M. soon saw the important role that Onn would play and many meetings between the two took place during the next few years.

M.M.'s impact on the 'establishment' in Singapore and Malaya was dramatic. He soon decided that dinner jackets would no longer be necessary when dining at his residence and this put the ladies in a bit of a quandary. Should they wear long or short? Many times I had to give advice on fashions – a duty which was really outside the responsibilities of a Private Secretary. Soon our guests got used to being met by the Governor-General in slacks, a short-sleeved silk shirt and a bow tie. I don't think the senior civil servants ever really came to terms with this 'short-sleeved democracy'.

There was considerable opposition amongst these senior civil servants to the constitutional changes which were being proposed. Not only were they resistant to change, desiring a return to the old status quo, but they saw, sooner or later, the end of their careers. In my case, a career in the Colonial Service which could have lasted to normal retirement age of fifty-five ended when I was thirty-nine.

Above all his other qualities, I believe M.M. was a supreme politician. He had great charm which he could turn on and off like water out of a tap.

He was a wonderful listener and never forgot a conversation. He was a master of the English language and often reminded me of Churchill in the way he spoke and his sparing use of words. Often he would dictate a long despatch and ask that it be produced, double-spaced, in draft so that he could correct it. It used to come back for 'fair copy and transmission' with the absolute minimum of corrections and alterations.

I remember on one occasion he asked me what was the latest time that a cable could be sent from Singapore to Whitehall to be decoded and delivered. It was some time in the early evening and I asked whether I could not send it earlier as I was quite keen to put in a few holes of golf before it got dark. 'No,' he said, 'you must postpone such a decision until the last possible moment. The position could change after you had sent the despatch and then you would look a fool.' I think he knew that he would be regarded in the future as a man of great stature; every article of correspondence, important or trivial, had a copy made for his personal file.

The social side of life in the Governor-General's household was extremely pleasant. When he was High Commissioner in Canada, M.M. had met and married the widow of Colonel Rowley, a distinguished Canadian soldier. After a time she arrived with her two children; she was young, charming and extremely good-looking. I don't think she was all that interested in the politics of the work but she was a very wonderful hostess and very kind to me and my friends. The private secretaries and A.D.C.s were known as 'the flunkeys' union'. The children were full of life and soon had the household staff looking after their every need. I don't think M.M. appreciated what it would be like having youngsters tearing round the corridors of his comparatively small residence. He always seemed quite glad to get to his office in the middle of Singapore.

Before Audrey MacDonald arrived, another Canadian and his charming wife took the post of Senior A.D.C. Major (soon to be Colonel) Jean-Paul Martin and his wife Renée had known M.M. in Ottawa and had accepted his invitation to come to Malaya. They were a great couple and we soon became the best of friends. Being new to the country and its peoples and traditions, they relied on me for a measure of guidance in the first few weeks but they were soon rushing ahead under their own steam. We shared a small bungalow not far from M.M.'s residence and very soon managed to establish an acceptable sharing of the vast number of duties and responsibilities. I don't think that a single cross word passed between us in all the time we were together – on the other hand, there were many hilarious occasions. When I finally retired from Malaya in 1960, it was wonderful to see the Martins again in their house in Quebec and a great sadness that Jean-Paul died soon afterwards. He had been seriously wounded in Italy at the battle of Cassino and the effects of the injury were always with him. But, he never complained and always saw the bright side of life.

Jean-Paul was a strong shoulder on which I could lean when things got a bit overpowering. He was much older than I was and, having known M.M. in Canada as a friend and not as a boss, was able to adopt a slightly different attitude to the one I was forced to follow. He would certainly question decisions if he thought a mistake was being made. It was amazing to see how quickly he established himself with Governors, Generals, Admirals and all the other top hamper of the establishment.

Chapter 21

People and Places

As I have said, it is not my intention to write a complete history of my time with Malcolm MacDonald but there were certain interesting people and places that are worth a 'snapshot'. I did not travel with him as much as the A.D.C. as I was usually left in Singapore to 'mind the shop'. But I did make two trips to Borneo and Sarawak.

M.M. had been at the centre of negotiations for the purchase of North Borneo from the North Borneo Company and I was lucky to go along with him when the hand-over took place. We arrived in a frigate of the Royal Navy which was very impressive but not very comfortable. These fighting ships were not really designed for such ceremonial occasions and I remember being very glad that we only spent one night on board. I was delighted to find that I was to stay with Chief Justice Brace, who had known my father in Nigeria. My face fell a bit when I found that my room was in a sort of summer house, roofed with palm fronds, in the garden. That first night there was a dreadful storm, lashing winds and tropical rain and I spent the whole time trying to keep myself and my kit dry.

The newly installed Governor, Sir Edward Twining, gave a dinner party in the evening and the proceedings were enlivened by M.M. walking in on his hands. He was a very good athlete and that was one of his party pieces; included was a descent of about four steps which always impressed me.

When we visited Sarawak M.M. decided that he would arrive from Labuan, an island not very far away, by small boat. He also decided that he would change into his full dress uniform with sword, plumed helmet, etc., etc., on the small boat. Imagine the consternation when it was discovered, just as the landing point came into view round a bend in the river, that someone had forgotten to pack the Governor-General's braces. All the other bits and pieces were there – uniform, white gloves, dress wellingtons – but no braces. So I sacrificed my braces and spent an uncomfortable afternoon hoping that my trousers would not fall down.

Kuching was a revelation, a wonderful palace on the riverbank and gentle people who were sad to see the end of the Brooke dynasty.

We had many visits from politicians in the U.K. and other important people; these put a considerable strain on our resources as we did not have many spare rooms and had to farm people out in Singapore. I well remember the visit of Field Marshal Viscount Montgomery who came to preside over a meeting of the Southeast Asia Defence Committee. Many words have been written about Monty and it would be quite inappropriate of me to presume to add to them; sufficient to say that I did not find him easy. We had to re-arrange all the cars so that he could have the Governor-General's Rolls Royce and on the way to the meeting he asked imperiously, 'Where is the other car?' When I said that there was no other car, he asked, 'What happens to me when this one breaks down?' I put forward the view that Rolls had a pretty good reputation for reliability but in the very unlikely event of a breakdown we would probably have to hitch a ride in the escorting police jeep. This did not please the great man and he ordered, 'Tomorrow, see that there is a second car!' This posed a bit of a problem for me because, just after the war, Singapore was not exactly flush with large limousines and I had already had to shuffle things around in order to get everyone in the household to their various destinations. But, we did have two very smart little black Austin 10s with silver crowns instead of number plates; these were used for delivering mail and other important duties such as taking the head cook to market. I ordered one of these to take post behind us when we set out on the morrow and, true to form, the Field Marshal asked, 'Where is the second car?' When I pointed out the post car, he exploded, 'You don't expect me to ride in that thing, do you?' 'No, sir,' I replied. 'I hope you will be able to continue to ride in the Rolls.' The upshot of the story is that M.M. called me to his office that evening and said, 'I hear you've been taking the "mickey" out of the Field Marshal about cars.' I think he was quite amused when I told him the whole story.

I suppose the most thrilling moment of all was our visit to India on the way home to the U.K., which was to be my last duty before handing over my responsibilities. From afar M.M. had watched the awful developments in India at the time of partition and accepted an invitation from the Mountbattens to stay with them on his way home for consultations in the Colonial Office in London. Lady Louis had stayed with us in Penang on one of her many tours in connection with her work for the Red Cross. She had been a personal friend of M.M. for some years.

I doubt if there are enough words in our language to describe the magnificence of Viceregal Lodge in New Delhi. It was huge and I remember I had to walk nearly a quarter of a mile to get from the main office to my bedroom. The imposing building, one of Lutyens' best known works, stands on a slight hill overlooking the city. The gardens were magnificent and the whole place staffed with hundreds of servants in their various grades and seniorities. One could not walk carrying a brief-case without a smartly dressed man coming quietly alongside saying, 'Sahib,' and taking the case. The bath in the morning and evening was run and the temperature tested by another shadow-like figure who moved around without making the slightest noise.

I remember being very impressed when the butter pats on a bed of ice on my breakfast tray were embossed with 'M of B', Mountbatten of Burma. But that was nothing compared with the splendour of the banquet for many of the Rulers which was held while we were there. The table, with its magnificent cutlery, china and glass seemed to stretch for miles. I was at one end with one of the A.D.C.s and next to me was Mr. Khrishna Menon, the Indian Ambassador in London. After dinner we all sat round in little groups and, with so many important people at the gathering, I was very surprised to be asked, 'At the next change round, Her Excellency would like to talk to you.' It was like musical chairs; when the word was given I went, straightening my tie as I walked, bowed, shook hands and sat down beside Lady Louis. I was a little taken aback when she said, 'I remember we have met before, it was not in Malaya and you were not dressed as you are now in a white dinner jacket.' After a few moments thought, she went on, 'I think it was in a camp in Manila and you were complaining that you were not getting home fast enough and that the Australians seemed to be getting priority.' That was an amazing feat of memory, it might have been possible for someone to tell her that I had been in a camp in Manila but no-one could possibly know about the conversation. She was interested to hear how I had finally got home and my impressions of my stay in India. She was a really wonderful person.

I suppose the high spot of our visit was the day when we had lunch with Jawaharlal Nehru and his daughter, Mrs. Indira Gandhi, and later in the day went to see Mahatma Gandhi. Lunch was at Nehru's residence and the four of us sat in a dark cool room. Nehru and Malcolm MacDonald were engrossed in conversation about the tremendous happenings in India at that time and Mrs. Gandhi was left to talk to me. I thought that she was one of the most beautiful and entrancing women that I had ever met. One felt immediately at ease with her and I remember telling her about myself and my life as though she was someone I had known for years. I enjoyed the lunch, even though the dishes were strange even to someone who had spent some years in the East.

I was introduced to Nehru but did not have long to talk to him. I recall being very ill at ease in his presence and I found it difficult to understand why. I suppose it was because one had read so much about him and his campaigns in opposition to the British in India. He had a striking face, fine features and piercing eyes and, as a product of Harrow and Cambridge, a great command of the language. I always regret that I was out of earshot and could not eavesdrop on the conversation between M.M. and Nehru.

It must have been about twelve days before he was assassinated when we went to see Mahatma Gandhi in Birla House, where he lived in New Delhi. There was a large garden with a raised platform in the middle and when we arrived Gandhi was sitting on a charpoi with his spinning wheel in front of him. He seemed so small and frail that one wondered how he had become such an influential figure in Indian politics. Not very many days previously he had broken a long fast which must have weakened him considerably but one felt that one was in the presence of a God-like being – even if he did resemble a little bird. I felt almost a personal loss when I read of his violent death so soon after we had seen him.

We left New Delhi in the comfort of the Viceroy's personal plane to join the scheduled flight back to London. A few days in the Colonial Office and then leave. During that leave I married the girl I had met two years previously and we returned to Malaya to a District Officer's posting just at the beginning of the Emergency – but that is another story.

Appendix

BUCKINGHAM PALACE

The Queen and I bid you a very warm welcome home.

Through all the great trials and sufferings which you have undergone at the hands of the Japanese, you and your comrades have been constantly in our thoughts. We know from the accounts we have already received how heavy those sufferings have been. We know also that these have been endured by you with the highest courage.

We mourn with you the deaths of so many of your gallant comrades.

With all our hearts, we hope that your return from captivity will bring you and your families a full measure of happiness, which you may long enjoy together.

George R.I.

September 1945.

Message from the Secretary of State for the Colonies

Welcome home. You have suffered a long and bitter ordeal at the hands of a barbarous enemy.

You have never been out of our thoughts and we now know, as we had always expected, that you have borne the ordeal with the spirit of your race.

That experience is now past and freedom is yours again. You may find in your homeland the scars of six years of war but you will not find any lack of goodwill and affection, and I wish you all good fortune in the future and a quick and full recovery to all whose health has suffered from their privations.

G. H. HALL.

[P.T.O.

COLONIAL OFFICE,
DOWNING STREET, S.W.1.

October, 1945

NOTE BY THE SECRETARY OF STATE

FOR THE COLONIES

I understand that disappointment has been expressed by members of the Government services of Malaya and Hong Kong who have been released from internment on the ground that arrangements have not been made for them to remain in or return immediately to their public functions in the territory in order to help in the restoration of normal administration. I sincerely appreciate the public spirit of these officers and am most grateful for their desire at once to take up an active part in the administration.

In planning the liberation and rehabilitation of the Far Eastern Colonial territories it was necessary to provide for unknown contingencies and it was decided, for reasons which I am sure will be generally appreciated, that the only safe course was for the forces of liberation to be prepared to establish a Military Administration of the countries in order to ensure the basis of law and order and full powers to adjust any emergency conditions which might be found or might develop in an initial phase. Staffs were assembled and sent out in accordance with this plan and while it is a matter for real gratification that so many of the released personnel are ready and willing to resume duty in the near future, I am sure that it is in the best interests, both of themselves and of the countries which they serve, that the initial phase should be carried out as planned and that they themselves should lose no time in obtaining rest and recuperation and of making contact once again with their families and friends before they are called upon to return to tackle the vast and difficult reconstruction problems which will confront the civil administrations at the next phase.

I have heard that some officers are under some apprehension lest on account of their absence their interests may be prejudiced and lest they may find that in the meantime others have secured the places which they might fairly have hoped to occupy. I can assure them that no grounds for such apprehension exist. All officers of the Government Services who are fit and able to return to duty after a holiday, will receive the full and sympathetic consideration which is due to them in the building up of the restored civil administrations.

G. H. HALL.

P/179954

4th April, 1946.

Sir,

Now that the time has come for your release from active military duty, I am commanded by the Army Council to express to you their thanks for the valuable services which you have rendered in the service of your country at a time of grave national emergency.

At the end of the emergency you will relinquish your commission, and at that time a notification will appear in the London Gazette (Supplement), granting you also the honorary rank of Captain. Meanwhile, you have permission to use that rank with effect from the date of your release.

I am, Sir,

Your obedient Servant,

Eic. B.B.Kurd.

Captain G.S. Patterson,
Royal Artillery.

Weight Chart

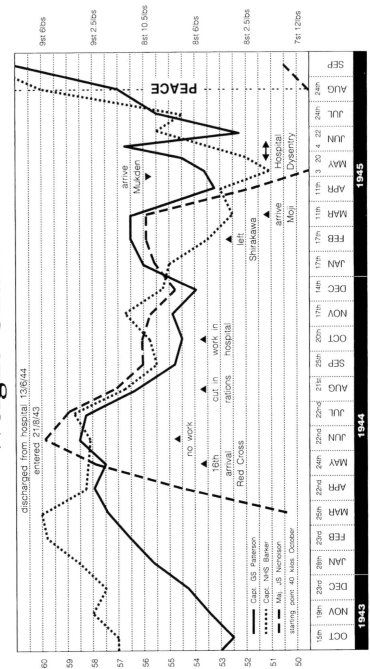

MAY—JUNE. 1942

JUNE. 1942